U0925342

Bilingual version of the illustrations 双语插图版

世界名人名言录

编　　译 / 宋雅丽
英文审读 / Hannah Boughton

山西出版集团
山西科学技术出版社

图书在版编目（CIP）数据

世界名人名言录/宋雅丽编译.—太原：山西科学技术出版社，2007.7

ISBN 978-7-5377-3026-6

Ⅰ.世… Ⅱ.宋… Ⅲ.①英语—汉语—对照读物②格言—汇编—世界 Ⅳ.H319.4：H

中国版本图书馆CIP数据核字（2007）第108762号

世界名人名言录

编　译：宋雅丽

出　版：山西出版集团·山西科学技术出版社

（太原建设南路21号　邮编：030012）

发　行：山西出版集团·山西科学技术出版社（电话：0351-4922121）

经　销：各地新华书店

印　刷：山西新华印业有限公司美术印刷分公司

开　本：850毫米×1168毫米　1/24

印　张：12

字　数：271千字

版　次：2007年8月第1版

印　次：2007年8月太原第1次印刷

书　号：ISBN 978-7-5377-3026-6

定　价：21.00元

如发现印、装质量问题，影响阅读，请与发行部联系调换。

版权所有，侵权必究！

Preface

This book is a compilation of many wonderful quotes said by people from around the world. Many of the people are famous for their contributions to the goodwill of mankind in cultures worldwide. Others are maybe not so famous, but their words are just as memorable. Rita has compiled this thorough list of useful quotes that will change your life.

I've been in China for many years. I like China very much and I have many Chinese friends. Rita was my student in Beijing. She is very diligent in her work and a thoughtful person. We often have discussions about eastern and western culture. We hope to add many wonderful things to your life.

July, 2007 in Beijing

编者的话

女儿的家庭作业需要每天收集两条名人名言，为此我翻出了中学时用过的一个本子，里面是那时候自己摘抄的满满的一本名人名言。本子的纸页已经泛黄，上面落满了灰尘，可是望着那熟悉的笔迹，让我想起了自己的中学时光，老师每天上课前在黑板上为我们抄下的那些句子；想起写作文、演讲时如何慷慨激昂地引用那些句子；想起了那些话曾经给自己的启迪与激励；想起了自己年少时的激情与梦想……它们在我的心灵中留下了难以磨灭的印象，甚至影响了我整个的人生。时隔二十多年，再细细品读那些充满了智慧与哲理的话语，仍然能被它们深深地打动。

现在的孩子课业远比我们那时候繁重，而且随着经济和科技的发展，获取信息的便捷，人们可能已经不会再花很多时间来抄写那些喜欢的东西了，但是总有一些会留下，也应该留下些什么，来作为自己人生的印迹。生命和时间如流水，悠悠向前，永不回头，幸好精神的领域不完全受其限制，能有这样一本书陪伴我们一生，会留下许多美好的记忆。

为此我们精选了世界范围内各领域杰出人物的名言佳句汇集成了这本书，其中尤其注重选取了原汁原味的英语原句，并采用了英汉对照的形式，不仅适用于各种层次的读者，而且便于对照学习、欣赏。为方便您记下生词和自己的心得体会，我们特意在页边留出了作笔记的地方。为了增加您的阅读兴趣，在书中附有100多位名人的图片及简介，不仅可以欣赏、可以珍藏，而且在学习语言、启迪心智的同时可以扩大知识面。

关于名言的分类，一直是仁者见仁、智者见智，因为同样一句话可能会蕴含着丰富的内涵，无法把它具体归入某一类别。所以我们根据自己的理解，按照从个体到整体的思路，将全书分为了六个篇章（感悟人生、做人的根本、让文化滋养心灵、在家中、事业与成功、与世界相连），每一篇章又分为若干个子类，以便于查阅。考虑到广大青少年读者的要求，我们根据新课标的理念加入了如何做人及合作、创新的条目，在大力提倡素质教育的今天，希望本书也能成为较好的学习辅助读本。

在每句名言后面，我们都提供了双语人名及国籍、身份介绍，这样可以加深相关单词的记忆，了解名人基本情况，但是有些名人在不同的领域都有杰出成就，我们无法一一列出，所以只采用了公众最认可的部分。

对于书中一些稍难的单词，我们曾想加以注释，但一是为版式的整齐美观；二是书中已采用了双语对照形式；最重要的是不能确定自己的选词是否能符合特定读者的需求，所以我们特意留出记笔记处，您可以自己从字典中查阅生词，记下感想，这样自主、互动地读书也许会更有收获。

在历史长河中留下来的名人名言浩如烟海，本书不可能全部收录，同时因为选编者的视角有限，可能与您的理解会稍有不同，为此我们特意留出几页，来记下您最喜欢的名人名言，让这本书真正成为您自己的朋友。

本书还有许多其他有趣之处，在这里就不一一赘述了，只要您打开它，就会发现有意外的惊喜与收获。

在本书的编写过程中，参考了其他一些选本、各类辞典及国外的大量报刊书籍等，在此一并向这些编译者表示感谢，如果涉及版权问题，请及时与我联系。由于编者水平有限，书中的疏漏和错误之处在所难免，希望您能提出宝贵意见，以便再版时改正。

Hannah 是我的英语老师，从她的身上，我学到了许多东西。在审读书稿的过程中，她对书的内容提出了许多中肯的建议，并提供了许多有用的资料。

编写此书的这段日子里，有太多的人给予了我无私的帮助与鼓励，在此我对他们致以最真诚的谢意，正是因为有了家人、朋友的爱与支持，才使我对生活充满了信心。

宋雅丽

2007 年夏

CONTENTS

第一辑　感悟人生
The Understanding of Life

幸福最重要的本质是：有所为、有所爱、有所希冀。

The grand essentials of happiness are：something to do，something to love，and something to hope for.

第二辑　做人的根本
The Fundamentals of Human Beings

品质之于人，犹如芳香之于鲜花。

Personality is to man what perfume is to a flower.

第三辑　让文化滋养心灵
Culture Nourishes the Mind

美的东西是永恒的喜悦。

A thing of beauty is a joy forever.

第四辑　在家中
Homelife

我们爱自己的家，我们的脚可以离它而去，可我们的心却不能。

We love our home, though our feet can leave it, yet our hearts cannot.

CONTENTS

第五辑　事业与成功
A Successful Career

如果一个人朝他的梦想自信地前进，为他所想象的生活努力，他将在平淡的生活中遇到意想不到的成功。

If one advances confidently in the direction of his dreams, and endeavors to live the life he has imagined, he will meet with a success unexpected in common hours.

第六辑　与世界相连
Connected with the World

我们都应当关心未来，因为我们今后的生活将在那里度过。

We should all be concerned about the future because we will have to spend the rest of our lives there.

The Under-standing of Life

感悟人生

幸福最重要的本质是：

有所为、

有所爱、

有所希冀。

The grand essentials of happiness are:

something to do,

something to love,

and something to hope for.

Oscar Wilde

王尔德（1854—1900），英国作家、戏剧家、诗人。他生于都柏林，毕业于牛津大学。虽然他主要以成人作家而著称，但他的早期作品中有两本童话集《快乐王子故事集》和《石榴之家》已载入英国儿童文学史册。在他事业的顶峰，最具代表性的是他的几部大戏，如《温德摩尔夫人的扇子》、《理想的丈夫》等，都是一时绝唱。也正是他的第一部童话集问世之后，人们才真正将他视为有影响力的作家。他机智过人、才华横溢，成为唯美主义的代表，并被誉为“才子和戏剧家”。

Kahlil Gibran

纪伯伦（1883—1931），黎巴嫩诗人、散文作家、画家。他生于黎巴嫩北部山乡卜舍里，曾在巴黎艺术学院学习绘画和雕塑，并得到艺术大师罗丹的奖掖，后在美国从事文学艺术创作，直至逝世。20世纪20年代初，以纪伯伦为代表形成的阿拉伯第一个文学流派“叙美派”曾闻名全球。文学与绘画是纪伯伦艺术生命的双翼。纪伯伦的前期创作以小说为主，后期创作则以散文诗为主。《先知》被认为是他的代表作，作者以智者临别赠言的方式，论述爱与美、生与死、婚姻与家庭、劳作与安乐、法律与自由、理智与热情、善恶与宗教等一系列人生和社会问题，充满了比喻和哲理，具有东方色彩。书中，纪伯伦自绘了充满浪漫情调和深刻寓意的插图。

Life
生活

To love oneself is the beginning of a life-long romance.

Oscar Wilde, British writer

爱自己是浪漫人生的开始。

——王尔德，英国作家

Where is the life we have lost in living?
Where is the wisdom we have lost in knowledge?
Where is the knowledge we have lost in information?

Thomas Steams Eliot, British poet and critic

在谋生中我们把生活丢到哪里去了？
在知识中我们把智慧丢到哪里去了？
在信息中我们把知识丢到哪里去了？

——艾略特，英国诗人、评论家

When life does not find a singer to sing her heart, she produces a philosopher to speak her mind.

Kahlil Gibran, Lebanese poet and novelist

当生活找不到歌唱家来歌唱她的心声时，她便创造了哲学家来倾诉她的思想。

——纪伯伦，黎巴嫩诗人、小说家

One of the sources of pride in being a human being is the ability to bear present frustrations in the interests of longer purposes.

Helen Lynd, American sociologist

人类引以自豪的理由之一是:具有为长远目标而忍受当前挫折的能力。

——海伦·林德,美国社会学家

So rich in life that its flowers perish and it is full of sadness.

Pablo Neruda, Chilean poet and diplomat

生命如此丰富,以致花朵枯萎,而且充满忧伤。

——聂鲁达,智利诗人、外交家

There are many wonderful things in nature, but the most wonderful of all is man.

Sophocles, Ancient Greek dramatist

自然界有许多美好的东西,但最美的是人。

——索福克勒斯,古希腊剧作家

The difference between ancients and moderns is that the ancients asked what we have experienced, and moderns asked what we can experience.

A. N. Whitehead,
British mathematician and philosopher

古人和今人的区别在于:古人追问"我们经历了什么",而今人追问"我们能经历什么"。

——怀特海,英国数学家、哲学家

Life is a one-way street, and we are not coming back.

Anonymous

人生是一条单行道,我们将永不回头。

——佚名

The tragedy of life is not what men suffer, but rather what they miss.

Thomas Carlyle, British historian and essayist

生活的悲剧不在于人们所经受的苦难,而在于他们所错过的一切。

——卡莱尔,英国历史学家、散文家

Life is made up of interruptions.

Sir William S. Gilbert, British dramatist and poet

生活是由坎坷构成的。

——吉尔伯特爵士,英国剧作家、诗人

Life is short, the art long, opportunity fleeting, experience treacherous, and judgement difficult.

Hippocrates, the Father of medicine

人生短暂,艺术漫长,机会稍纵即逝,经历险象环生,而判断也非轻而易举。

——希波克拉底,西方医学之父

I slept and dreamed that life was beauty; I woke and found that life was duty.

E. S. Hooper

我睡着时,梦见生活是美景;我醒来时,发现生活是责任。

——胡珀

The wine of life keeps oozing drop by drop;
The leaves of life keep falling one by one.

Omar Khayyám, Persian poet and astronomer

生命之酒一滴一滴渗出;
生命之叶一片一片飘落。

——海亚姆,波斯诗人、天文学家

A man lives not only his personal life as an individual, but also, consciously or unconsciously, the life of his epoch and his contemporaries.

Thomas Mann, German writer

一个人不仅作为个体过着自己的生活,而且有意无意地过着属于那个时代以及同时代人的生活。

——托马斯·曼,德国作家

It's always the way in this life. No sooner have you got settled in a pleasant resting place than you're summoned to move on.

Charlotte Brontë, British female writer

生活总是这样,你刚到一个令人愉快的休憩地,又有某种原因让你前行了。

——夏洛蒂·勃朗特,英国女作家

We do not choose to be born. We do not choose our parents. We do not choose our historical epoch, the country of our birth, or the immediate circumstances of our upbringing. We do not, most of us, choose to die; nor do we choose the time or conditions of our death. But within all this realm of choicelessness, we do choose how we shall live: courageously or in cowardice, honorably or dishonorably, with purpose or in drift. We decide what is important and what is trivial in life. We decide that what makes us significant is either what we do or what we refuse to do. But no matter how indifferent the universe may be to our choices and decisions, these choices and decisions are ours to make. We decide. We choose. And as we decide and choose, so are our lives formed. In the end, forming our own destiny is what ambition is about.

Jaseph Epstein, American essayist and editor

我们无法选择出身和父母,也无法选择出生的历史时期、国家或成长环境。我们中的大部分人都不能选择死亡,更不能选择死亡的时间或者条件。但是,在这些无法选择的领域,我们可以选择怎样活着:是勇敢无畏地活着,还是战战兢兢地生存;是活得光明磊落,还是卑鄙无耻;是目标坚定,还是随波逐流。我们要权衡生活中的轻重缓急,选择让生命更具有意义的事情,决定我们要做的事或拒绝做的事。但是,不论世界如何漠视我们所做出的选择,那些的确是我们自己做出的决定。总之,我们的抉择构成了我们的生活,我们命运的构筑正取决于抱负的全部内容。

——爱波斯坦,美国散文作家、编辑

Three passions have governed my life: the longing for love, the search for knowledge, and unbearable pity for the suffering of humankind.

Bertrand Russell, British philosopher

三种激情控制着我的生活：对爱的渴望，对知识的寻求，还有对人类苦难难以抑制的同情。

——罗素，英国哲学家

I have suffered and despaired and known death and I am glad that I am in this great world.

Rabindranath Tagore, Indian poet

我曾经痛苦、绝望，曾经体会死亡，然而生活在这个伟大的世界上，我感到欢畅。

——泰戈尔，印度诗人

What makes life dreary is the want of motive.

George Eliot, British female writer

生活所以变得沉闷是因为缺乏人生的目标。

——乔治·艾略特，英国女作家

Sooner or later, we must realize there is no station, no one place to arrive at once and for all. The true joy of life is the trip. The station is only a dream. It constantly outdistances us.

Robert J. Hastings, American writer

迟早，我们会意识到人生没有终点站，没有什么地方真正完美。生命的真正乐趣在于旅行的过程。终点站只是一个梦，它永远在我们的前方。

——黑斯廷斯，美国作家

Rabindranath Tagore

泰戈尔（1861—1941），印度诗人、小说家、社会活动家。他出生于加尔各答市，曾留学英国学习法律和文学，运用孟加拉语和英语从事文学创作。泰戈尔是具有巨大世界影响力的作家，他共写了50多部诗集，被称为“诗圣”。他还写了大量文学、哲学、政治论著，并创作了1500多幅画，谱写了许多歌曲。他的主要作品有抒情诗集《吉檀迦利》、《飞鸟集》、《新月集》，长篇小说《戈拉》、《沉船》和短篇小说《摩诃摩耶》、《素芭》等。1913年，获诺贝尔文学奖，他是亚洲第一个诺贝尔文学奖获得者。

Bertrand Russell

伯特兰·罗素（1872—1970），英国哲学家、数学家和社会活动家。他出身于威尔斯一贵族家庭。18岁进入剑桥大学三一学院，师从著名数学家、哲学家怀特海。毕业后，留校任教。1921年，他曾来中国讲学。他的代表作为哲学著作《西方哲学史》、《心的分析》、《物的分析》、《哲学问题》，社会学随笔《婚姻与道德》、《一个自由人的崇拜》、《我为什么不是一个基督徒》等。1950年，他获得了诺贝尔文学奖。

Victor Hugo

雨果（1802—1885）是法国浪漫主义作家的代表人物，19 世纪前期积极浪漫主义文学运动的领袖，法国文学史上卓越的资产阶级民主作家。他出生于法国贝桑松，曾在巴黎和马德里接受教育。14 岁时，他写出第一部剧本，此后继续写作。雨果几乎经历了 19 世纪法国的一切重大事变。他一生写过多部诗歌、小说、剧本及各种散文、文艺评论和政论文章，成为 19 世纪法国最多产的作家。其代表作有《巴黎圣母院》、《悲惨世界》等。

Henry David Thoreau

梭罗（1817—1862），美国作家、思想家。他生长在波士顿附近超验主义思想运动中心康科德村，20 岁于哈佛大学毕业，在爱默生影响下，阅读柯尔律治、卡莱尔等人的著作，研究东方的哲学思想，形成了一套独立见解。自 1845 年起，他蛰居于自建在瓦尔登湖畔的林中小屋，在那里写成堪称美国文学经典之作的《瓦尔登湖》。在他笔下，自然、人以及超验主义理想交融汇合，浑然一体。他是 19 世纪超验主义运动的重要代表人物。梭罗的文章简练有力、朴实自然，富有思想内容，在美国 19 世纪散文中独树一帜。

Life is “trying things to see if they work”.

Ray Bradbury, American writer of science fiction

生活就是尝试各种事物,看是否行得通。

——布拉德伯里,美国科幻小说家

The important thing in life is to have a great aim, and the determination to attain it.

Goethe, German writer

人生的重要事情是确定一个伟大目标,并矢志去实现它。

——歌德,德国作家

However mean your life is, meet it and live it: do not shun it and call it hard names. Things do not change, we change.

H. D. Thoreau, American writer and thinker

无论你的生活多么恶劣,勇敢地面对它:不能回避和诅咒它。生活不会改变,只有我们改变。

——梭罗,美国作家、思想家

The broadest in the world is sea, the sky is broader than sea, man's mind broader than the sky.

Hugo, French writer

世界上最宽阔的是海洋,比海洋更宽阔的是天空,比天空更宽阔的是人的胸怀。

——雨果,法国作家

Life is just a series of trying to make up your mind.

T. Fuller, British clergyman and historian

生活只是由一系列下决心的努力所构成的。

——富勒,英国牧师、历史学家

Good friends, good books and a sleepy conscience: this is the ideal life.

Mark Twain, American writer

拥有良书、益友和一颗宁静的心:这就是理想的生活。

——马克·吐温,美国作家

Trifles make the sum of life.

Charles Dickens, British writer

琐事组成生活。

——狄更斯,英国作家

Life is like an onion: you peel it off one layer at a time, and sometimes you weep.

Carl Sandburg, American writer

生活像一个洋葱,你只能一层一层把它剥开,有时你还得流泪。

——卡尔·桑德伯格,美国作家

We think in generalities, but we live in detail.

A. N. Whitehead,

British mathematician and philosopher

我们思考事物的普遍原理,但我们却生活在细节中。

——怀特海,英国数学家、哲学家

While there is one untrodden tract for intellect or will, and men are free to think and act, life is worth living.

A. Austin, British writer and The Poet Laureate

只要还有一块知识和意志尚未征服的领域,只要人们能自由地思考和行动,生活就是值得的。

——奥斯汀,英国作家、桂冠诗人

There are two kinds of people: those who take things positively, and those who think pessimistically. Each group of people enjoy themselves in their own way.

KENZABURO OE,
Japanese Nobel Prize-winning writer

世界上有两种人:乐观行事的人和悲观思考的人。每一种人都欣赏自己的处事方式。

——大江健三郎,诺贝尔奖获得者、日本作家

Life is not fair, get used to it.

William (Bill) H. Gates, Chairman of Microsoft

生活是不公平的,要去适应它。

——比尔·盖茨,美国微软公司董事长

Life is the enjoyment of emotion, derived from the past and aimed at the future.

A. N. Whitehead, British
mathematician and philosopher

追思过去,憧憬未来,生命是一种情感的享受。

——怀特海,英国数学家、哲学家

Self-reverence, self-knowledge, self-control, these three alone lead life to sovereign power.

A. Tennyson, British poet

自尊、自知、自制,这三点即可将生命引向无限生机。

——丁尼生,英国诗人

The poverty of goods is easily cured; the poverty of the soul is irreparable.

Montaigne, French thinker and essayist

物品的匮乏很容易弥补,精神的贫瘠无可挽救。

——蒙田,法国思想家、散文家

If wrinkles must be written upon our brows, let them not be written upon the heart. The spirit should not grow old.

James Garfield, American President

如果皱纹不得不写在额上,请一定不要把它们写在心里。精神应当永远不老。

——加菲尔德,美国总统

The trees reflected in the river—they are unconscious of a spiritual world so near them. So are we.

Nathaniel Hawthorne, American writer

倒映在河中的树影,意识不到精神世界离它们那么近,我们也是如此。

——霍桑,美国作家

Life might be a glorious adventure, but is turned into a horrible experience and all this happens because human existence so far has been entirely dominated by fear. For fear, I repeat it, is at the bottom of all intolerance.

Hendrik Willem Van Loon, American writer

生活本应该是一次光荣的冒险,结果却变成了一个可怕的经历。之所以如此,就是因为迄今为止人类的生存完全被恐惧控制着。我要重复一遍,所有不宽容的根源,都是恐惧。

——房龙,美国作家

Life has value only when it has something valuable as its object.

George Hegel, German philosopher

生活仅当存在有价值的目标时才具有意义。

——黑格尔,德国哲学家

Anyone can carry his burden, however hard, until nightfall. Anyone can do his work, however hard, for one day. Anyone can live sweetly, patiently, lovingly, purely, till the sun goes down. This is all that life really means.

Robert Louis Stevenson, British novelist

任何人的负荷,不论如何沉重,他都能负担到日暮时分。任何人的工作,不论如何艰辛,他都可以支撑着做一整天。任何人都能甜美地、耐心地、可爱地、纯洁地生活下去,直到日落。这就是人生的全部真实底蕴。

——史蒂文森,英国小说家

Human life is everywhere a state in which much is to be endured, and little to be enjoyed.

Samuel Johnson, British writer

人生处处要多忍受,少享受。

——塞缪尔·约翰逊,英国作家

Keep your face always towards the sunshine, and the shadows will fall behind you.

Walt Whitman, British poet

永远面对阳光,阴影自然会抛在后面。

——惠特曼,英国诗人

Life finds its wealth by the claims of the world, and its worth by claims of love.

Rabindranath Tagore, Indian poet

人生因世界对它的要求而变得丰富,因爱心对它的要求而有了价值。

——泰戈尔,印度诗人

The world is like a mirror; frown at it and it frowns at you; smile and it smiles too.

Samuel Johnson, British writer

世界如一面镜子:皱着眉看它,它也皱眉看你;你笑着对它,它也笑着看你。

——塞缪尔·约翰逊,英国作家

If life cheats you, neither be worried nor be anxious. Believe that happy days will yet arrive.

Alexander Pushkin, Russian poet

假如生活欺骗了你,不要忧虑,不要心急。相信吧,快乐的日子将会来临。

——普希金,俄国诗人

Life is indeed darkness save when there is urge, and all urge is blind save when there is knowledge, and all knowledge is vain save when there is work, and all work is empty save when there is love.

Kahlil Gibran, Lebanese poet and novelist

生活的确是黑暗的,除非有了希冀;所有的希冀都是盲目的,除非有了知识;所有的知识都是无用的,除非有了工作;所有的工作都是空洞的,除非有了爱。

——纪伯伦,黎巴嫩诗人、小说家

Happiness
幸福

There is only one happiness in life, to love and be loved.

George Sand, French female writer

人生中只有一种幸福:爱和被爱。

——乔治·桑,法国女作家

The supreme happiness of life is the conviction that we are loved.

V. Hugo, French writer

生命中最大的幸福就是坚信有人爱我们。

——雨果,法国作家

It's pretty hard to tell what does bring happiness. Poverty and wealth have both failed.

Elbert Hubbard, American writer

很难说什么能带来幸福,贫穷和财富都没能带来幸福。

——哈伯德,美国作家

The grand essentials of happiness are: something to do, something to love, and something to hope for.

Allan K. Chalmers, American writer

幸福最重要的本质是:有所为,有所爱,有所希冀。

——艾伦·K. 查默斯,美国作家

A man can hope for satisfaction and fulfillment only in what he does not yet possess; he cannot find pleasure in something of which he has already too much.

Carl Jung, Swiss psychiatrist

人只有在还没有拥有的事物中才有希望得到满足,在已拥有的太多的事物中是不可能发现乐趣的。

——荣格,瑞士精神病学家

Just as a cautious businessman avoids investing all his capital in one concern, so wisdom would probably admonish us also not to anticipate all our happiness from one quarter alone.

Sigmund Freud, Austrian psychologist

正如谨慎的商人避免将所有的资金投入一项事业,古训告诫我们不可仅从一方面期待幸福。

——弗洛伊德,奥地利心理学家

The foundation of true happiness is in the conscience.

L. A. Seneca, Ancient Roman philosopher

幸福的真正根本在于良心。

——塞内加,古罗马哲学家

Man is fond of counting his troubles, but he does not count his joys. If he counted them up as he ought to, he would see that every lot has enough happiness provided for it.

Dostoyevsky, Russian writer

人们喜欢数落自己的苦处,却不考虑自己的快乐。如果把这些进行合理的统计,他会看到每个人都拥有命运赋予的足够的幸福。

——陀思妥耶夫斯基,俄国作家

海伦与沙利文

Helen Keller

海伦·凯勒（1880—1968），美国作家。她出生于亚拉巴马州，19 个月时因生病丧失视听能力，但她跟随沙利文小姐学习，沙利文教她说话、读书、写字，并陪伴了她一生。她于 1904 年获得学位，进而成为著名的演讲家和作家。1902 年，她发表自传《我的一生》，该书后由吉布森改写成剧本《奇迹创造者》，获普利策奖。

Hendrik Willem Van Loon

房龙（1882—1944），荷裔美国作家。他出生于荷兰鹿特丹，1903 年赴美，在康奈尔大学完成本科学业。1911 年，他获德国慕尼黑大学博士学位后，曾在美国几所大学任教，后任记者、编辑和播音员等。1921 年，《人类的故事》的出版使他一举成名。他在历史、文化、文明、科学等方面都有著作，而且读者众多。早在 20 世纪 30 年代，房龙的部分著作即被译成中文出版，影响了当时整整一代年轻人。房龙的著作，其选题基本上围绕人类生存发展的最本质的问题，其目的是向人类的无知与偏执挑战，普及知识与真理，使之成为人所共知的常识，因而具有历史不衰的魅力。其主要作品有《宽容》、《文明的开端》、《人类的家园》、《奇迹与人》、《圣经的故事》等。

Sorrows remembered sweeten present joy.

Jackson Pollock, American artist

不忘过去的痛苦,才能倍感今天的幸福。

——波洛克,美国艺术家

When one door of happiness closes, another opens, but often we look so long at the closed door that we do not see the one which has been opened for us.

Helen Keller, American writer

当一扇幸福之门关闭,另一扇将会打开。但是,我们常常死死盯着那扇关闭的门以至于看不到另一扇为我们而开的门。

——海伦·凯勒,美国作家

Everyone could find salvation after his own fashion.

Hendrik Willem Van Loon, American writer

每个人都可以按自己的方式获得拯救。

——房龙,美国作家

Happiness is a perfume you cannot pour on others without getting a few drops on yourself.

Ralph Waldo Emerson, American thinker

幸福犹如香水,你不可能泼向别人而自己却不沾几滴。

——爱默生,美国思想家

The greatest happiness is to know the source of unhappiness.

Dostoyevsky, Russian writer

最大的幸福是懂得不幸的根源。

——陀思妥耶夫斯基,俄国作家

Fortune, seeing that she could not make fools wise, has made them lucky.

Montaigne, French thinker and essayist

幸运之神看出来她无法使傻子聪明,于是她就使傻子幸福(傻人有傻福)。

——蒙田,法国思想家、散文家

Happiness lies not in the mere possession of money; it lies in the joy of achievement, in the thrill of creative effort.

Franklin Roosevelt, American President

幸福不在于拥有金钱,而在于获得成就时的喜悦以及产生创造力的激情。

——富兰克林·罗斯福,美国总统

If one only wished to be happy, this could be easily accomplished; but we wish to be happier than other people, and this is always difficult, for we believe others to be happier than they are.

Montesquieu, French philosopher and jurist

如果你仅仅希冀幸福,这不难做到;但我们期望比别人更幸福,这总是难于做到,因为我们认为别人会比实际更幸福。

——孟德斯鸠,法国哲学家、法理学家

Ideal
理想

The ideals which have lighted my way, and time after time have given me new courage to face life cheerfully, have been Kindness, Beauty, and Truth.

Albert Einstein, American scientist

有些理想曾经为我指引过道路,并不断给我新的勇气以欣然面对人生,那些理想就是——真、善、美。

——爱因斯坦,美国科学家

The ideal is in thyself, the impediment too is in thyself.

Thomas Carlyle, British historian and essayist

理想存在于你自身,障碍亦存在于你自身。

——托马斯·卡莱尔,英国历史学家、散文家

It is only in marriage with the world that our ideals can bear fruit; divorced from it, they remain barren.

Bertrand Russell, British philosopher

只有与现实联姻,我们的理想才能结果。倘若脱离现实,理想将永无生机。

——罗素,英国哲学家

The only limit to our realization of tomorrow will be our doubts of today.

Franklin Roosevelt, American President

实现明天理想的唯一障碍是今天的疑虑。

——富兰克林·罗斯福,美国总统

Ideals are like the stars, we never reach them, but like mariners, we chart our course by them.

Carl Schurz, American statesman

理想就像天上的星星,我们永远够不着,但我们像水手一样需要靠它来指引航程。

——舒尔茨,美国政治家

If you really want something you can figure out how to make it happen.

Cher, American actress and singer

如果你真的想要一个东西,你就能想出如何得到它。

——雪儿,美国女演员、歌手

A man is not old as long as he is seeking something; a man is not old until regrets take the place of dreams.

J. Barrymore, American actor

一个人只要还有所追求,就依然年轻;直到悔恨代替了梦想,他才算老。

——巴里莫尔,美国演员

Cher

雪儿（1946— ），原名Cherylin Sarkisian LaPiere，美国女歌手、演员。她出身于加利福尼亚州一个贫穷的单亲家庭，靠偶尔在电影中饰演小角色和卖唱为生。16岁时，她去洛杉矶学习表演与演唱，并取得好成绩。20世纪70年代中期以后，她把更多的精力放在了表演事业中，并于1987年凭借在《Moonstruck》中令人信服的演技，获得了第60届奥斯卡最佳女主角奖。20世纪90年代后，她的事业不但没有下滑，反而在1999年凭借《Believe》获得了第42届格莱美奖最佳舞曲专辑奖。1998年底，她出版了回忆录“*The First Time*”。

雪儿于1999年获格莱美奖的专辑封面

John Barrymore

巴里莫尔（1882—1942），美国演员，被称为“伟大的形象”（The Great Profile）。他出生于美国宾夕法尼亚州的费城，以扮演莎士比亚剧中人物成名，尤以饰演哈姆雷特最为著名，同时他还因私人的动荡生活而引人注目。他的古典式鼻子与出众的外貌，使他得到上边的称号。他演出的最后一部电影名叫《伟大的形象》。

Mark Twain

马克·吐温（1835—1910），美国作家、新闻记者和演说家。他生于密苏里州佛罗里达，当过印刷工人，后来在密西西比河上当领航员，他的笔名 Mark Twain 就取自水手报告河水深浅时的回答声（英文意为“水深两浔”）。随后，他还做过编辑、记者，并赴国外游历，之后写成《傻子国外旅行记》，该书为他博得了“幽默作家”的美称。他的代表作《汤姆·索亚历险记》、《哈克贝里·费恩历险记》都取材于作者本人的童年经历，牢固地确立了其世界经典之作的地位。他还是一位知名度很高的演说家，所到之处追随者如潮。

Romain Rolland

罗曼·罗兰（1866—1944），法国近代杰出的批判现实主义作家、音乐史学家、社会活动家和政论家。他出身于巴黎附近的克拉姆西镇一个律师家庭。1895 年，获得罗马的法国考古学校博士学位后，他在巴黎高等师范学校和巴黎大学讲授艺术史，从事文学创作，兼写音乐评论。第一次世界大战期间，他移居瑞士，坚持反战立场，第二次世界大战期间，在沦陷的法国闭门著书，直至巴黎光复。他的代表作是长篇巨著《约翰·克利斯朵夫》和《母与子》，中篇小说《彼埃尔和吕丝》，戏剧《丹东》、《爱与死的搏斗》、《罗伯斯庇尔》等。此外，他还撰写了名人传记《贝多芬传》、《米开朗琪罗传》、《托尔斯泰传》和《甘地传》等。他于 1915 年获诺贝尔文学奖。

One can never consent to creep when one feels an impulse to soar.

Helen Keller, American writer

当你有翱翔的冲动时,千万不要同意爬行。

——海伦·凯勒,美国作家

Everybody sets out to do something, and everybody does something, but no one does what he sets out to do.

George Moore, British novelist

人人都有理想,人人都在努力,但没有一个人做的是他最初想要做的事。

——乔治·穆尔,英国小说家

Keep away from people who try to belittle your ambitions. Small people always do that, but the really great make you feel that you, too, can become great.

Mark Twain, American writer

远离那些贬低别人理想的人,小人总是贬低别人的理想。真正伟大的人让你觉得你也可以成为伟大的人。

——马克·吐温,美国作家

Realism without ideals is meaningless, and idealism away from reality is lifeless.

Romain Rolland, French writer

缺乏理想的现实主义是毫无意义的,脱离现实的理想主义是没有生命的。

——罗曼·罗兰,法国作家

Ideal is the beacon. Without ideal, there is no secure direction; without direction, there is no life.

Leo Tolstoy, Russian writer

理想是指路明灯。没有理想,就没有坚定的方向;没有方向,就没有生活。

——托尔斯泰,俄国作家

Between the ideal and the reality, between the motion and the act, falls the shadow.

Thomas Stearns Eliot, British poet and critic

理想与现实之间,动机与行为之间,总有一道阴影。

——艾略特,英国诗人、评论家

Man can survive only when he has the substance; man can live only when he has ideal. Do you want to know the difference between survival and life? Animals survive, while men live.

T. Hughes, British poet

人有物质才能生存,人有理想才能生活。你想知道生存与生活的不同吗?动物生存,而人生活。

——休斯,英国诗人

Hope
希望

Miracles happen everyday. Somebody doesn't think so but they do. You've to get to put the past behind you before you can move on.

Winston Groom, American novelist

每天都有奇迹发生。虽然有人不相信,但它们的确在发生。在你继续前进之前,你必须将过去抛在脑后。

——温斯顿·格罗姆,美国小说家

We must accept finite disappointment, but we must never lose infinite hope.

Martin Luther King,
American civil-rights leader

我们必须接受失望,因为它是有限的;但千万不可失去希望,因为它是无限的。

——马丁·路德·金,美国民权运动领导人

Property is not without any fears and disasters, and adversity is not without comforts and hopes.

Francis Bacon,
British essayist and philosopher

幸运中并非不掺杂各种担心与灾难,而厄运中也并非不存在欣慰与希望。

——培根,英国散文作家、哲学家

Percy Bysshe Shelley

雪莱（1792—1822），英国著名诗人。他于20岁进入牛津大学，投身社会后，积极支持民族解放斗争，1822年渡海遇风暴不幸船沉溺死。雪莱是跟拜伦齐名的欧洲著名浪漫主义诗人。其作品热情而富哲理思辨，诗风自由不羁。其最优秀的作品有长诗《仙后麦布》，抒情故事诗《伊斯兰的反叛》，政治诗《暴政的行列》、《自由颂》，表现革命热情及胜利信念的《西风颂》，以及取材于古希腊神话的表现人民反暴政胜利后瞻望空想社会主义前景的代表诗剧《解放了的普罗米修斯》等。

Friedrich Nietzsche

尼采（1844—1900），德国哲学家。他出生于德国勒肯，自幼性情孤僻、自卑，因此一生都在追寻一种强有力的人生哲学来弥补自己内心深处的自卑感。1865年，他进入莱比锡大学攻读古典语言学，并开始接触叔本华的哲学思想。他以第一部著作《悲剧的诞生》献给他的朋友瓦格纳，认为后者的歌剧是希腊悲剧的真正继承者。他决心赋予他那个时代以新的价值观，把叔本华的“权力意志”奉为基本信条。他的重要著作《查拉图斯特拉如是说》发展了“超人”的思想，对存在主义具有重大影响。1889年，长期不被人理解的尼采由于无法忍受孤独而失去理智，1900年去世。

If winter comes, can spring be far behind?

Percy Bysshe Shelley, British poet

冬天来了,春天还会远吗?

——雪莱,英国诗人

A strong hope is more inspiring to life than any pleasure already realized.

Friedrich Nietzsche, German philosopher

强烈的希望,比任何一种已实现的快乐,对人生具有更大的激励作用。

——尼采,德国哲学家

Our hopes, often though they deceive us, lead us pleasantly along the path of life.

La Rochefoucauld, French writer

希望尽管时常欺骗我们,却引导着我们愉快地走过人生之路。

——拉罗什富科,法国作家

All men live in hope.

Jane Austen, British female writer

人人都靠希望生存。

——简·奥斯汀,英国女作家

He who has never hoped can never despair.

George Bernard Shaw, British dramatist

从来没有抱什么希望的人也永远不会失望。

——萧伯纳,英国剧作家

We grow weary of those things (and perhaps soonest) which we most desire.

Samuel Butler, British poet

我们最容易(也可能最快地)厌倦我们最渴望的东西。

——塞缪尔·巴特勒,英国诗人

Freedom

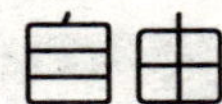

Whenever you have an aim, you must sacrifice something of freedom to attain it.

William Somerset Maugham, British novelist

当你有一个目标,就得牺牲一定的自由去实现它。

——毛姆,英国小说家

Liberty means responsibility. That is why most men dread it.

George Bernard Shaw, British dramatist

自由意味着责任,正因为如此,多数人都惧怕自由。

——萧伯纳,英国剧作家

Set the bird's wings with gold and it will never again soar in the sky.

Rabindranath Tagore, Indian poet

鸟儿的翅膀缀上了黄金,再也不能翱翔在蓝天上。

——泰戈尔,印度诗人

The only man who is really free is the one who can turn down an invitation to dinner without giving any excuse.

Jules Renard, French playwright and novelist

唯一真正自由的人是能够拒绝宴会的邀请而不用找借口的人。

——勒纳尔,法国剧作家、小说家

Jean Jacques Rousseau

卢梭（1712—1778），法国哲学家、作家。他出生于瑞士日内瓦，自学成才，从事过多种职业。1754年，他撰写了《论人类不平等的起源和基础》。1757年，他迁居卢森堡，写出杰作《社会契约论》，提出了“自由、平等、博爱”的口号，对法国的革命思想产生了巨大的影响。其代表作有《忏悔录》、教育论著《爱弥儿》等。

Johann Wolfgang Von Goethe

歌德（1749—1832），德国作家。他出生于法兰克福市，从小受文学熏陶，兴趣广泛。他除了有诗歌、戏剧和小说等创作外，在解剖学和植物学方面也有一定的成就。1774年，歌德的浪漫小说《少年维特之烦恼》问世，轰动了文坛，他也因此闻名于欧洲文学界。歌德最著名的作品是《浮士德》，诗剧反映的是人类追求生命意义的伟大精神，从构思到完成，前后共经历了60年。正是此书，奠定了歌德在世界文学史上的崇高地位。

The sum of behavior is to retain a man's own dignity, without intruding upon the liberty of others.

Francis Bacon, British essayist and philosopher

人的行为准则是:维护自己的尊严,又不妨碍他人的自由。

——培根,英国散文作家、哲学家

There is in liberty as in innocence and virtue a satisfaction one can only feel in their enjoyment and a pleasure which can cease only when lost.

Jean Jacques Rousseau, French philosopher

自由同清白与美德一样,只有在你享有它们时,才感到满足,一旦失去它们,你就会感到欢乐停止了。

——卢梭,法国哲学家

A light heart can bear anything!

Johann Wolfgang Von Goethe, German writer

一颗轻松的心能承受任何事情!

——歌德,德国作家

It is better to be free and poor than to have everything you want and have to do what someone tells you all the time.

Aesop, Ancient Greek fable writer

与其拥有所需要的一切而时刻听命于他人,还不如贫穷而自由。

——伊索,古希腊寓言作家

None can love freedom heartily, but good men; the rest love not freedom, but license.

John Milton, British poet

只有善良的人才钟爱自由;其他的人不是爱自由,而是爱放纵。

——弥尔顿,英国诗人

None is of freedom or of life deserving unless he daily conquers it anew.

Johann Wolfgang Von Goethe, German writer

只有每天为生活与自由拼搏的人,才配享受生活与自由。

——歌德,德国作家

Freedom is more important than comfort.

Aesop, Ancient Greek fable writer

自由比舒适更重要。

——伊索,古希腊寓言作家

Only he is free who cultivates his own thoughts, and strives without fear of man to do justice to them.

Berthold Auerbach, German novelist

只有培育自己思想的人才是自由的人,他们勇往直前,不担心别人对自己评价是否公正。

——奥尔巴克,德国小说家

Dream

梦想

There is nothing like a dream to create the future.

Victor Hugo, French writer

没有什么比梦想更能创造未来。

——雨果，法国作家

Yesterday is but today's memory, and tomorrow is today's dream.

Kahlil Gibran, Lebanese poet and novelist

昨天只是今天的记忆，而明天是今天的梦想。

——纪伯伦，黎巴嫩诗人、小说家

Nothing happens unless first a dream.

Carl Sandburg, American writer

什么都不会发生，除非先有梦想。

——桑德伯格，美国作家

The work goes on, the cause endures, the hope still lives and the dreams shall never die.

Edward Kennedy, American senator

工作进行，事业持久，希望尚存，梦想不死。

——肯尼迪，美国参议员

Martin Luther King

马丁·路德·金（1929—1968），美国民权运动领袖。他出生于佐治亚州亚特兰大，曾就读于克罗泽尔神学院和波士顿大学，是黑人民权运动的领导人，他以非暴力反抗政策和受欢迎的演讲技巧而著称于世。1963 年，他在华盛顿林肯纪念堂前向和平进军的 25 万人发表了著名的演说——“我有一个梦想”，为反对种族歧视、争取平等发出呼号。1964 年，他获得肯尼迪和平奖和诺贝尔和平奖。他的最大成就在于对美国南方的种族隔离法规进行了挑战，后在田纳西州孟菲斯市遇刺身亡。

No one should negotiate their dreams. Dreams must be free to flee and fly high, no government, no legislature, has a right to limit your dreams. You should never agree to surrender your dreams.

Jesse Jackson, American civil-rights leader

谁都不能买卖他的梦想。梦想必须自由来去,展翅高飞。任何政府、法律都无权限制你的梦想。你决不应放弃你的梦想。

——杰克逊,美国民权运动家

What is now proved was once only imagined.

William Blake, British poet

现在被证实了的在过去曾是梦想。

——布莱克,英国诗人

I have a dream that one day this nation will rise up and live out the true meaning of its creed:We hold these truths to be self-evident,that all men are created equal.

Martin Luther King, American civil-rights leader

我有一个梦想,有那么一天,我们这个民族将会奋起反抗,并且坚持它的信条的真谛,这是不言自明的——那就是人人生而平等。

——马丁·路德·金,美国民权运动领袖

Struggle
奋斗

Cease to struggle and you cease to live.

Thomas Carlyle, British writer

生命不止,奋斗不息。

——卡莱尔,英国作家

Man cannot discover new oceans unless he has courage to lose sight of the shore.

André Gide, French writer

人只有鼓起勇气告别海岸,才能发现新的海洋。

——纪德,法国作家

Luck is a dividend of sweat. The more you sweat, the luckier you get.

Ray A. Kroc, American businessman

运气是汗水的红利,你流的汗越多,你就越幸运。

——克洛克,美国实业家

Whatever you can do or dream, you can begin it. Boldness has genius, power and magic in it.

Johann Wolfgang Von Goethe, German writer

无论你做什么或梦想什么,你都可以开始,勇气中含有天赋、能力和魔力。

——歌德,德国作家

Ray A. Kroc

克洛克（1902—1984），美国实业家，麦当劳快餐连锁店的创始人。20世纪50年代，他是泡沫奶油搅拌机生产商，对其用户麦克和迪克·麦当劳（Mac and Dick McDonald）通过街摊销售汉堡包、炸薯条的标准经营方式印象深刻，他买下了街摊的经营权，就质量、卫生、服务和价格制定出严格的标准，并实行各餐馆经营者特许经销管理制，取得了巨大的成功。1959年，他开办了第100家麦当劳快餐连锁店，1967年开设第一家海外分店。

André Gide

纪德（1869—1951），法国20世纪最重要的作家之一。他生于巴黎，11岁时丧父，由母亲扶养并给予清教徒式的教育，造就了他的叛逆性格。他受尼采主义的影响，全面扬弃传统道德观念，宣扬独立、自由。纪德的文学创作走的是一条探索之路，作品充满矛盾，表现人们普遍关注的问题。其代表作有《人间粮食》、《背德者》、《伪币制造者》、《如果种子不死》，以及游记和日记。纪德的作品文笔清丽精湛，思想深邃细腻，语言温婉和谐，具有古典美。他于1947年获得诺贝尔文学奖。

Life is thickly sown with thorns, and I know no other remedy that to pass quickly through them. The longer we dwell on our misfortunes; the greatest is their power to harm us.

Voltaire, French thinker

人生布满了荆棘，我所晓得的唯一办法是从那些荆棘上面迅速踏过。我们对于自己所遭遇的不幸想得越多，它们对我们的伤害就越大。

——伏尔泰，法国思想家

Do not linger to gather flowers to keep them, but walk on, for flowers will keep themselves blooming all your way.

Rabindranath Tagore, Indian poet

不要为采撷花朵而驻足流连，只管前行，一路上鲜花自会不断绽放。

——泰戈尔，印度诗人

A man dies still if he has done nothing, as one who has done much.

Homer, Ancient Greek poet

无所事事亦难逃一死，不如奋斗终生。

——荷马，古希腊诗人

One should want only thing and want it constantly. Then one is sure of getting it.

André Gide, French writer

人必须只渴望得到一件东西，并且不断地怀着这种渴望，那么他必然会得到它。

——纪德，法国作家

Work accomplished means little. It is in the past. What we all want is the glorious and living present.

Sherwood Anderson, American writer

已完成的事几乎没有意义，它属于过去；我们大家都需要的是充满生命力的壮丽的现在。

——谢伍德·安德逊，美国作家

They who lose today may win tomorrow.

Cervantes, Spanish writer

今天失手的人或许明天又能赢回来。

——塞万提斯，西班牙作家

Miracles sometimes occur, but one has to work terribly for them.

Chaim Azriel Weizmann, Israel President

奇迹有时候是会发生的，但是你得为之拼命地努力。

——魏茨曼，以色列总统

When a man is willing and eager, God joins in.

Aeschylus, Ancient Greek dramatist

当人自愿且热衷于某事时，神也会助他。

——埃斯库罗斯，古希腊剧作家

The man who has made up his mind to win will never say "impossible".

Bonaparte Napoleon, French Emperor

凡是决心取得胜利的人从来不说"不可能"。

——拿破仑，法国皇帝

That which is bitter to endure may be sweet to remember.

Thomas Fuller, *British clergyman and historian*

那些痛苦的经历也许是甜蜜的回忆。

——托马斯·富勒,英国牧师、历史学家

The future does not belong to those who are indecisive, but to those who once the decision is made will strive hard towards the goal and will never give up until reaching the goal.

Romain Rolland, *French writer*

未来并不属于那些犹豫不决的人,而是属于那些一旦决定之后,就不屈不挠、不达目的誓不罢休的人。

——罗曼·罗兰,法国作家

Love
爱情

Life is a flower of which love is the honey.

Victor Hugo, French writer

人生是花朵,爱情是花蜜。

——雨果,法国作家

The love that lasts longest is the love that is never returned.

W. S. Maugham, British novelist

永恒的爱是无须回报的爱。

——毛姆,英国小说家

It is certainly true that nothing in the world makes a person indispensable but love.

Johann Wolfgang Von Goethe, German writer

世界上只有爱才能使你成为一个不可缺少的人。

——歌德,德国作家

Love is not love when it is mingled with regards that stand apart from the entire point.

William Shakespeare, British dramatist and poet

爱情里面要是夹杂了和它本身无关的算计,那就不是真正的爱情。

——莎士比亚,英国剧作家、诗人

Oh, love is real enough, you will find it some day but it has one archenemy, and that is life.

Jean Anouilh, French dramatist

啊,爱情是多么真实,可是有一天你会发现,爱情有一个大敌,那就是生活。

——让·昂韦,法国剧作家

Love, and a cough, cannot be hid.

George Herbert, British poet

爱和咳嗽一样都无法隐藏。

——赫伯特,英国诗人

How changeable are the feelings of mankind in different environments! What we love today always turns out to be what we hated; what we pursue today always turns out to be what we shall try to shun; what we aspire for today always turns out to be what we shall be afraid of or even shudder before.

Daniel Defoe, British writer

在不同的环境中,人类的情感怎样变幻无常啊! 我们今天所爱的,往往会成为我们所恨的;我们今天所追求的,往往是我们明天所逃避的;我们今天所渴望的,往往是我们明天所害怕的,甚至是胆战心惊的。

——笛福,英国作家

But there's nothing half so sweet in life as love's young dream.

Thomas Moore, Irish poet

一生中没有任何事情能够赶得上年轻的爱情之梦一半甘甜。

——托马斯·穆尔，爱尔兰诗人

A man falls in love through his eyes, a woman through her ears.

W. Wyatt

男人用眼睛去爱，女人则用耳朵去爱。

——怀亚特

Will you love me in the good old-fashioned way?
When my hair has all turned grey.
Will you kiss me then and say.
That you love in December as you do in May?

John Walker,
British Rhyming Dictionary compilationist

你是否还会用那美好的过去的方式爱我，
当我满头华发的时候？
你是否还会用吻来告诉我，
你将爱我如初？

——约翰·沃克，英国韵律辞典编纂家

Every man is a poet when he is in love.

Plato, Ancient Greek philosopher

每个恋爱中的人都是诗人。

——柏拉图，古希腊哲学家

One should hold fast one's heart; for when one let it go, how quickly doth one's head run away!

Friedrich Nietzsche, German philosopher

必须牢牢控制感情,因为一旦撒手,理智飞快失去!

——尼采,德国哲学家

Love brings ecstasy and relieves loneliness.

Bertrand Russell, British philosopher

爱带来狂喜,减轻孤独。

——罗素,英国哲学家

Love has a thousand ways to please, but more to rob us of our ease.

John Dryden, British critic and dramatist,
The Poet Laureate

爱情有千种方法令人愉快,但有万种方法让人不安。

——德莱顿,英国评论家、剧作家,桂冠诗人

First love is only a little foolishness and a lot of curiosity.

George Bernard Shaw, British dramatist

初恋就是一点点笨拙外加许许多多好奇。

——萧伯纳,英国剧作家

Love sees with the heart and not the mind; therefore, winged Cupid is painted blind.

William Shakespeare, British dramatist and poet

爱是用心而非脑去看。因此,长翅膀的爱神丘比特被画成了盲人。

——莎士比亚,英国戏剧家、诗人

A mother takes twenty years to make a man of her boy, and another woman makes a fool of him in twenty minutes.

Robert Frost, American poet

母亲花20年才能把一个男孩子造就成男子汉，而另一个女人花20分钟就能把他变成傻子。

——罗伯特·弗罗斯特，美国诗人

Love never dies a natural death. It dies because we don't know how to replenish its source. It dies of blindness and errors and betrayals. It dies of illness and wounds. It dies of weariness, of withering, of tarnishing.

Anais Nin, French-born American female writer

爱从不自然消亡。它逝去是因为我们不懂如何补充它的源头，是因为盲目、过失和背叛，是因为疾病和创伤，是因为厌烦、凋零和暗淡。

——宁，法裔美国女作家

Human nature is so constructed that it gives affection most readily to those who seem least to demand it.

Bertrand Russell, British philosopher

人性就是如此，它最乐意将爱给予那些似乎最不强求爱的人。

——罗素，英国哲学家

A lady's imagination jumps from admiration, to love, to marriage, in a moment.

Jane Austen, British female writer

女人的想象力是跳跃式的，从爱慕到相爱到结婚，一会儿的事。

——简·奥斯汀，英国女作家

The man often hopes he is the object of the woman's initial love, while the woman hopes she is the last romance of the man.

Oscar Wilde, British writer

男人经常希望自己是女人的初恋对象,女人则希望成为男人最后的罗曼史。

——王尔德,英国作家

The greater one's love for a person, the less room for flattery. The proof of true love is to be unsparing in criticism.

Moliére, French dramatist

爱一个人爱得越深就越少恭维他,毫无保留的批评才验证真的感情。

——莫里哀,法国剧作家

You are the sunshine of my life; that's why I'll always stay around.

Stevie Wonder, American singer and instrumentalist

你是我生命的阳光,所以我永远呆在你的身旁。

——史蒂威·旺德,美国黑人歌唱家、器乐演奏家

Love is so short; forgetting is so long.

Pablo Neruda, Chilean poet and diplomat

爱情太短,而遗忘太长。

——聂鲁达,智利诗人、外交家

Stevie Wonder

史蒂威·旺德（1950— ），美国黑人歌唱家、器乐演奏家。他生于密执安州，生来双目失明，自幼接触和演奏各种乐器。1961年，他与莫汤唱片公司签约，他的第一张唱片《小史蒂威·旺德——12岁的天才》一问世即告成功。1971年，他与公司重新签订合同，获得对自己作品进行艺术处理的完全控制权。20世纪70年代，他成为最精通电子合成技术的艺术家之一。其主要唱片有《生命关头之歌》、《有声读物》、《内心视觉》和《火热胜七月》等。

Pablo Neruda

聂鲁达（1904—1973），本世纪最伟大的拉丁美洲诗人，智利外交家。他出身于帕拉尔城一铁路工人家庭，就读于圣地亚哥智利教育学院，曾任驻外使节和国会议员。他早期写格律诗，后改写自由体诗。在聂鲁达近半个世纪的文学创作中，情诗一直是他最脍炙人口的主题，也使得聂鲁达的名字几乎成为情诗的代名词。其代表作有抒情诗集《二十首情诗和一首绝望的歌》、《大地的居所》、《元素之歌》、《漫游与归来》等。他的作品手法夸张、情感浓烈、词汇丰富，具有很强的艺术感染力。他于1971年获诺贝尔文学奖。

You are like nobody since I love you.

Pablo Neruda, Chilean poet and diplomat

你与任何人都不同,因为我爱你。

——聂鲁达,智利诗人、外交家

Ever has it been that love knows not its own depth until the hour of separation.

Kahlil Gibran, Lebanese poet and novelist

每当别离时,方知爱有多深。

——纪伯伦,黎巴嫩诗人、小说家

Friendship
友谊

Without confidence, there is no friendship.

Epictetus, Ancient Roman philosopher

没有信任,就没有友谊。

——爱比克泰德,古罗马哲学家

The only reward of virtue is virtue; the only way to have a friend is to be one.

Ralph Waldo Emerson, American thinker

报答美德的唯一办法是还报以美德;找到朋友的唯一办法是自己成为别人的朋友。

——爱默生,美国思想家

Wishing to be friends is quick work, but friendship is a slow ripening fruit.

Aristotle, Ancient Greek philosopher

结交朋友只在一念之间,友谊却是慢慢成熟的果实。

——亚里士多德,古希腊哲学家

All the splendor in the world is not worth a good friend.

Voltaire, French thinker

人世间所有的荣华富贵比不上一个好朋友。

——伏尔泰,法国思想家

Betraying a trust is a very quick and painful way to terminate a friendship.

Ralph Waldo Emerson, American thinker

背叛会迅速而痛苦地断送友谊。

——爱默生，美国思想家

Friendship is an essential ingredient in the making of a healthful, rewarding life.

Ralph Waldo Emerson, American thinker

友谊是人生健康而有意义所不可缺少的部分。

——爱默生，美国思想家

Some components of a thriving friendship are honesty, naturalness, thoughtfulness, and some common interests.

Ralph Waldo Emerson, American thinker

确保友谊常青的诸要素是诚实、朴实自然、体贴和某些共同的兴趣。

——爱默生，美国思想家

If all the world hated you, and believed you wicked, while your own conscience approved you and absolved you from guilt, you would not be without friends.

Charlotte Bronté, British female writer

即使整个世界恨你，认为你很坏，只要你自己问心无愧，知道你是清白的，你就不会没有朋友。

——夏洛蒂·勃朗特，英国女作家

Ralph Waldo Emerson

爱默生（1803—1882），美国伟大的思想家、散文家和诗人，美国超验主义的旗手，在19世纪美国思想史、文化史和文学史上占有十分重要的地位。他出生于马萨诸塞州波士顿，哈佛大学毕业后一度教书，1834年移居康科德，与梭罗是师生兼朋友。他推崇精神和直觉，强调人的主观能动性，呼吁当时的美国人摆脱传统的束缚，创造具有本土特色的文化，被尊为“塑造美国人心灵的”一代思想宗师。其代表作有《论自然》、《美国学者》、《论自助》、《随笔》等。

Charlotte Bronté

夏洛蒂·勃朗特，与安妮·勃朗特（Anne Bronté）、艾米莉·勃朗特（Emily Bronté）并称为“文学三姐妹”。她们出生于英国约克郡山区，后在姨母的资助下，夏洛蒂与艾米莉一起去意大利进修法语和德语。她在意大利学习的经历激发了其表现自我的强烈愿望，促使她投身于文学创作的道路。其成名作《简·爱》写于1846年，她借一个出身寒微的年轻女子奋斗的经历，抒发了自己胸中的积愫，深深打动了当时的读者。《简·爱》的独特之处不仅在于小说的真实性和强烈的感染力，还在于小说塑造了一个不屈服于世俗压力、独立自主、积极进取的女性形象。

True friendship is like sound health; the value of it is seldom known until it is lost.

Charles Colton, British writer

真正的友谊犹如健康,只有失去时才会意识到它的价值。

——科尔顿,英国作家

The shifts of fortune test the reliability of friends.

Cicero, Ancient Roman statesman and orator

命运的变化考验朋友是否可靠。

——西塞罗,古罗马政治家、演说家

Friend: one who knows all about you and loves you just the same.

Elbert Hubbard, American writer

朋友是清楚地了解你以后依然爱你的人。

——哈伯德,美国作家

It takes your enemy and your friend working together to hurt you to the heart; the one to slander you and the other to get the news to you.

Mark Twain, American writer

你的敌人和朋友需要齐心协力才能把你的心伤透:敌人诽谤你,朋友把消息带给你。

——马克·吐温,美国作家

A real friend is one who walks in when the rest of the world walks out.

Walter Winchell,
American newspaper and radio commentator

真正的朋友是在其他人都弃你而去时走向你的人。

——沃尔特·温切尔,美国报纸、广播评论员

Two persons cannot long be friends if they cannot forgive each other's little failings.

Jean de La Bruyere, French moralist

如果两个人不能原谅彼此的小缺点,他们的友谊便不能持久。

——拉布吕耶尔,法国伦理学家

To be capable of steady friendship or lasting love, are the two greatest proofs, not only of goodness of heart, but of strength of mind.

William Hazlitt, British critic and essayist

稳固的友谊和持久的爱情,这两者是善良和睿智的明证。

——黑兹利特,英国评论家、散文作家

Without friends no one would choose to live, though he had all other goods.

Aristotle, Ancient Greek philosopher

一个人如果没有朋友,即使拥有其他一切,也不愿活下去。

——亚里士多德,古希腊哲学家

You can tell what people are like from the friends they choose.

Aesop, Ancient Greek fable writer

从人们所交的朋友可以看出他们是怎样的人。

——伊索,古希腊寓言作家

A friend that you buy with presents will be bought from you.

Thomas Fuller, British clergyman and historian

用礼物"买来"的朋友终会被买走。

——富勒,英国牧师、历史学家

It is well, when one is judging a friend, to remember that he is judging you with the same godlike and superior impartiality.

Arnold Bennett, British novelist

当你评价一个朋友的时候,最好记住他也正在以同样神圣而至高无上的公正在评价着你。

——阿诺德·本涅特,英国小说家

Throughout life, we rely on small groups of people for love, admiration, respect, moral support, and help.

Ralph Waldo Emerson, American thinker

整个一生,我们都有赖于从一些人群中获得友爱、赏识、尊敬、道义的支持和帮助。

——爱默生,美国思想家

To young people, friends are the advisors to remind them not to make mistakes; to old people, friends are the assistants to add to their strength in exhaustion and to take care of them in difficulty in life; to middle-age people, friends are the arms to help them accomplish their great causes.

Aristotle, Ancient Greek philosopher

对年轻人来说,朋友是提醒他们不犯错误的谋士;对老年人来说,朋友是补充他们衰竭体力、照顾他们生活困难的助手;对中年人来说,朋友是辅佐他们完成宏伟事业的臂膀。

——亚里士多德,古希腊哲学家

Pleasure
快乐

He is a wise man who does not grieve for the things which he has not, but rejoices for those which he has.

Epictetus, Ancient Roman philosopher

智者只为自己拥有的快乐,不为自己没有的伤心。

——爱比克泰德,古罗马哲学家

One of the greatest pleasures in life is conversation.

Logan Peasall Smith, American writer

生活中最大的乐趣之一是交谈。

——史密斯,美国作家

Grief can take care of itself, but to get the full value of joy you must have somebody to divide it with.

Mark Twain, American writer

悲伤可以独自承受,但欢乐必须与人分享才能领略到它的全部价值。

——马克·吐温,美国作家

Labor is often the father of pleasure.

Voltaire, French thinker

劳动常常是快乐之父。

——伏尔泰,法国思想家

The greatest pleasure I know, is to do a good action by stealth, and to have it found out by accident.

Charles Lamb, British essayist

据我所知,最大的乐趣是暗中做好事又偶被发现。

——兰姆,英国散文家

That man is the richest whose pleasures are the cheapest.

Herry David Thoreau,

American writer and thinker

能处处发现快乐的人才是最富有的人。

——梭罗,美国作家、思想家

The pleasure of all reading is doubled when one lives with another who shares the same books.

Katherine Mansfield, British female writer

当你和一个人住在一起,共享相同的书籍,一切快乐将会加倍。

——凯瑟林·曼斯菲尔德,英国女作家

If you change your mind—from pessimism to optimism—you can change your life.

Claipe Safran

如果你转变思想——从悲观主义者变为乐观主义者——你就能改变你的人生。

——克雷普·萨弗兰

We human beings often complain that there are so few good days and so many bad ones; but I think we are generally wrong. If our hearts were always open to enjoy the good, which God gives us every day, then we should also have enough strength to bear the evil, whenever it comes.

Johann Wolfgang Von Goethe, *German writer*

我们人类常常抱怨好时光如此之少,而坏日子又如此之多,我以为此论并不正确。如果我们总能敞开心胸,接受上帝每日赐予我们的快乐,那我们也应有足够的力量承受无论何时袭来的邪恶。

——歌德,德国作家

Sorrow

悲伤

Tell him who is anxious that this will not last. As happiness passes, so passes anxiety.

The Arabian Nights

告诉忧心忡忡的人,这是不会长久的,正如幸福会消失,不幸也会消散。

——《天方夜谭》

Character cannot be developed in ease and quiet. Only through experience of trial and suffering can the soul be strengthened, vision cleared, ambition inspired, and success achieved.

Helen Keller, *American writer*

安逸、平和不能使性格得以发展,只有经受痛苦的考验,才能加强心智、开阔眼界、鼓舞雄心壮志并且取得成功。

——海伦·凯勒,美国作家

If you shed tears when you miss the sun, you also miss the stars.

Rabindranath Tagore, *Indian poet*

假如,因错过太阳而哭泣,那么,你还会错过繁星。

——泰戈尔,印度诗人

Arthur Schopenhauer

叔本华（1788—1860），德国哲学家，生于波兰格但斯克，就读于格丁根大学和柏林大学。1820年，他在柏林大学任教，曾勇敢地与对立的黑格尔同时讲课，但吸引不了学生。后来，他迁居法兰克福，专事学术研究。其主要著作有《意志和表象的世界》，他把各种短论和格言式作品以《附录和补遗》为题结集出版，最终引起世人的注目。叔本华不仅影响了尼采、萨特等诸多哲学家，开启了非理性主义哲学，而且还影响了一大批作家和艺术家。

Michel de Montaigne

蒙田（1533—1592），法国伟大的思想家、作家，是一位独具个性的人文主义者。他出身新贵族，早期在波尔多大学学习，后攻读法律，当过15个文官，38岁回到庄园过退隐生活，开始撰写随笔。《蒙田随笔》行文旁征博引，语言平易晓畅，形象亲切生动，富于生活情趣。蒙田的创作开创了随笔这一体裁的先河，使散文作品进入了文学殿堂，同时也奠定了他在世界文学史上不可替代的地位。

The pain of the mind is worse than the pain of the body.

Publius Syrus, Syrian writer

心灵之痛远甚于身体之痛。

——赛勒斯,叙利亚作家

Sorrow and trouble either soften the heart or harden it.

James Mackintosh, British writer

悲哀和烦恼不是使人软弱,就是使人坚强。

——麦金托什,英国作家

A man who fears suffering is already suffering from what he fears.

Michel de Montaigne, French thinker and essayist

害怕痛苦的人已经在承受他所害怕的痛苦了。

——蒙田,法国思想家、散文家

A certain amount of care or pain or trouble is necessary for every man at all times. A ship without a ballast is unstable and will not go straight.

Arthur Schopenhauer, German philosopher

一定的担忧、痛苦或烦恼对每个人在任何时候都是必需的。一艘船如果没有压舱物,便不稳定,不能一直前行。

——叔本华,德国哲学家

He best can pity who has felt the sorrow.

John Gay, British dramatist and poet

感受过悲伤的人最富有同情心。

——盖伊,英国剧作家、诗人

What's the use of worrying? It never was worthwhile. So, pack up your troubles in your old kit bag, and smile, smile, smile.

George Asaf, British poet

担忧又有什么用？不值得。把烦恼塞进行囊，然后微笑、微笑、再微笑。

——阿萨夫，英国诗人

It is a sad truth that everyone is a bore to someone.

Arthur Miller, American dramatist

一个让人悲哀的事实是每个人都会让某个人感到厌烦。

——阿瑟·米勒，美国剧作家

Here is a rule to remember in the future, when anything tempts you to feel bitter: not "This is a misfortune", but "To bear this worthily is good fortune."

Marcus Aurelius, Ancient Roman Emperor

当有些事让你痛苦不堪时，将此规则铭记在心：不要想"这真是件不幸的事"，而应该认为"能够承受此事将是多么幸运"。

——马可·奥勒利乌斯，古罗马皇帝

Death
死亡

And so I leave this world, where the heart must either break or turn to lead.

Nicolas Chamfort, French writer

因此我要离开这个世界,这里要么让人心碎,要么让人心变硬。

——尚福,法国作家

Death is just the part of life. Somewhere all is destined to do.

Winston Groom, American novelist

死亡本来就是人生命的一部分。所有一切都在冥冥之中注定。

——温斯顿·格罗姆,美国小说家

In the midst of life we are in death.

Alighieri Dante, Italian poet

我们在生命中时时面对死亡。

——但丁,意大利诗人

We do not know what to do with this short life, yet we want another which will be eternal.

Anatole France, French novelist and critic

短短的此生我们都不知道该怎样度过,我们竟然还想要一个永恒的来生。

——法朗士,法国小说家、文艺评论家

A life of action and danger moderates the dread of death . It not only gives us fortitude to bear pain ,but teaches us at every step the precarious tenure on which we hold our present being.

William Hazllit, British critic and essayist

充满行动和危险的生活将减缓对死亡的恐惧。它不仅赋予我们承受痛苦的刚毅,而且时刻引导我们把握飘忽不定的现在。

——黑兹利特,英国评论家、散文家

No man should be afraid to die who hath understood what it is to live.

Thomas Fuller, British clergyman and historian

懂得了生的人,不应当怕死。

——托马斯·富勒,英国牧师、历史学家

It is not death that alarms me, but dying.

Michel de Montaigne, French thinker and essayist

让我们惊恐的不是死亡,而是死亡的过程。

——蒙田,法国思想家、散文家

Desire is half of life; indifference is half of death.

Kahlil Gibran, Lebanese poet and novelist

生命的一半是欲望;死亡的一半是冷漠。

——纪伯伦,黎巴嫩诗人、小说家

A dying man can do nothing easy.

Benjamin Franklin,

American statesman, writer, and scientist

一个临终的人做什么都不轻松。

——本杰明·富兰克林，

美国政治家、作家、科学家

If you would not be forgotten as soon as you are dead, either write things worth reading or do things worth writing.

Benjamin Franklin,

American statesman, writer, and scientist

如果你不想死后马上被遗忘，你要么写值得读的东西，要么做值得写的事。

——本杰明·富兰克林，

美国政治家、作家、科学家

Where life is more terrible than death, it is then the truest valor to dare to live.

Sir Thomas Browne, British writer and physician

当生比死还要可怕的时候，勇敢地活下去才是最真实的勇气。

——托马斯·布朗爵士，英国作家、医生

There is no cure for birth and death save to enjoy the interval.

G. Santayana, American philosopher and poet

人们对于生和死都无能为力，只有享受两者之间的间隙。

——乔治·桑塔亚那，美国哲学家、诗人

Carl Gustav Jung

荣格（1875—1961），瑞士心理学家，分析心理学的创立者。他出身于一个新教牧师的家庭，1900 年在巴塞耳大学获取医学博士学位，后在苏黎世大学的精神病学研究所任职。荣格是一个智力早熟的人，他性格孤僻，想象力丰富，博览群书。早期，他曾和弗洛伊德合作。后来，由于观点的不同，两人的关系最终破裂。他独树一帜的心理学理论及类型理论赢得了当时乃至今天世人的普遍认同和赞誉，从而成为了与弗洛伊德比肩而立的世界级心理学大师。他的分析心理学中的集体无意识理论可以解释其他心理学流派所无法解释的现象，如宗教问题、神话、象征、超感官知觉等。他把众多的人类活动都包含在这一理论之中，在历史、文学、人类学、宗教以及临床心理学领域产生了深刻而无比深远的影响。

D. H. Lawrence

劳伦斯（1885—1930），英国作家，同时也是一位颇有争议的作家。他出生于英国诺丁汉郡，就读于诺丁汉大学，当过小学校长，但因疾病和第一部小说《白孔雀》的小小成功而放弃执教从事写作。其主要作品有《儿子与情人》、《虹》、《查泰莱夫人的情人》等。他在英国文学史上的地位堪与现代主义文学大师詹姆斯·乔伊斯相提并论。他和乔伊斯的出现使英国现代主义小说进入了高峰时期。他的大多数作品通过对人内心世界的探索，表现性使人冲破障碍，而达到完成自我的主题。

To the psychiatrist, an old man who cannot bid farewell to life appears as feeble and sickly as a young man who is unable to embrace it.

Carl Gustav Jung, Swiss psychiatrist

对精神病医生来说，一个不能告别生活的老人与一个不能拥抱生活的年轻人同样是病态的、意志薄弱的。

——荣格，瑞士精神病学家

Death is the only pure, beautiful conclusion of a great passion.

D. H. Lawrence, British writer

死是伟大激情唯一纯洁而美丽的终结。

——劳伦斯，英国作家

我喜欢的名人名言

Some of my favorite quotes that are not contained in this book are:

我喜欢的名人名言

Some of my favorite quotes that are not contained in this book are:

The Fundamentals of Human Beings

做人的根本

品质之于人，

犹如芳香之于鲜花。

Personality is to man

what perfume is to

a flower.

Virtues

美德

Conscience is the inner voice that warns us somebody may be looking.

H. L. Mencken, American arts critic and linguist

良心是心灵的声音,警告我们说有人在注视着我们。

——门肯,美国文艺评论家、语言学家

A good listener is not only popular everywhere, but after a while, he knows something.

Wilson Mizner, American screenwriter

一个善于倾听的人不仅处处受欢迎,而且处处有收获。

——威尔逊·米兹纳,美国编剧

We have two ears and only one tongue so that we would listen more and talk less.

Diogenes, Ancient Greek philosopher

我们长两只耳朵,只有一个舌头,就是要我们多听少说。

——第欧根尼,古希腊哲学家

It is great to be great, but it is greater to be human.

W. Rogers, American humorist

成为伟人是美好的,做一个真正的人更美好。

——罗杰斯,美国幽默作家

He had not the good breeding to see that simplicity and naturalness are the truest marks of distinction.

William Somerset Maugham, British novelist

缺乏良好教养的人无法明白朴素和自然标志着最真实的高贵。

——毛姆,英国小说家

Goodness is achieved not in a vacuum, but in the company of other men, attended by love.

Saul Bellow, American novelist

善不是在真空而是在待人中体现,它需要用爱来滋润。

——索尔·贝娄,美国小说家

It is easy to perform a good action, but not easy to acquire a settled habit of performing such actions.

Aristotle, Ancient Greek philosopher

做一次好事很容易,然而养成为善的习惯并不容易。

——亚里士多德,古希腊哲学家

Patience and fortitude conquer all things.

Ralph Waldo Emerson, American thinker

忍耐和毅力征服一切。

——爱默生,美国思想家

Pretending to be something you are not may get you into trouble.

Aesop, Ancient Greek fable writer

伪装可能使自己陷入困境。

——伊索,古希腊寓言作家

La Rochefoucauld

拉罗什富科（1613—1680），法国经典作家。他生于巴黎，一生因爱情纠葛和政治阴谋被迫过着流亡生活。后参加投石党内战，受伤后退休回乡。他的《回忆录》在退休期间完成，但引起普遍争议。他的作品《反响录：警句与伦理箴言》最为著名，该书被通称为《箴言录》，使他成为法国文学中“箴言”的杰出代表。

Benjamin Franklin

本杰明·富兰克林（1706—1790），是资本主义精神最完美的代表，18世纪美国最伟大的科学家，著名的政治家和文学家。他出身贫寒，只受过两年的传统教育，却凭借自身的努力，成为了成功的商人、杰出的科学家和卓越的政治家。富兰克林首创了“共读社”，后来发展为美国哲学会，成为美国科学思想的中心。他签署了《独立宣言》，帮助起草了美国宪法，并成功赢得了法国和欧洲人民的支持，从而帮助美国人民赢得了独立战争。富兰克林还非常具有好奇心，他积极探索闪电等自然现象的奥秘，为后人留下了诸如避雷针等创造发明。

If you hear that someone is speaking ill of you, instead of trying to defend yourself, you should say "He obviously does not know me very well, since there are so many other faults he could have mentioned."

Epictetus, Ancient Roman philosopher

如果你听到有人说你的坏话,不要为自己辩护,反而要说:"他显然不太了解我,因为我还有许多别的毛病他没有提到。"

——爱比克泰德,古罗马哲学家

If we had no faults of our own we would not take so much pleasure in noticing those of others.

La Rochefoucauld, French writer

如果我们自身没有缺点,我们就不会如此乐此不疲地关注别人的缺点。

——拉罗什富科,法国作家

To show resentment at a reproach is to acknowledge that one may have deserved it.

Tacitus, Ancient Roman historian

对某一指责表示不满就是承认这一指责有可能是对的。

——塔西佗,古罗马历史学家

If you would be loved, love and be lovable.

Benjamin Franklin,
American statesman, writer, and scientist

如果你想被人爱,就要去爱别人,并让自己可爱。

——本杰明·富兰克林,
美国政治家、作家、科学家

He who tells a lie is not sensible of how great a task he undertakes; for he must be forced to invent twenty more to maintain that one.

Alexander Pope, British poet

一个撒谎的人往往意识不到他在执行一项多么伟大的任务;因为为了维持一个谎言,他就必须再编出20个谎言来。

——蒲柏,英国诗人

Civility costs nothing and buys everything.

Lady Mary Wortley Montagu, British female writer

礼貌没有任何代价,却可以买到一切。

——蒙塔古夫人,英国女作家

Everything ought to be beautiful in a human being: face, and dress, and soul, and ideas.

Anton Chekhov, Russian writer

人的一切——面貌、衣着、心灵和思想,都应该是美好的。

——契诃夫,俄国作家

There are only two sources of human vice—idleness and superstition, and only two virtues—activity and intelligence.

Leo Tolstoy, Russian writer

人类的罪恶之源只有两个——游手好闲和迷信;善行也只有两种——活动和智慧。

——列夫·托尔斯泰,俄国作家

Anton Chekhov

契诃夫（1860—1904），俄国作家，与法国作家莫泊桑、美国的欧·亨利并称为世界三大短篇小说作家。契诃夫出身于俄国一个杂货店老板家。父亲的杂货铺破产后，他靠做家庭教师维持生活和求学。1884 年，他从莫斯科大学医学系毕业后当了一名医生。与社会和人民的广泛接触，丰富了他的阅历，为日后的创作积累了素材。在 20 多年的创作活动中，他共写了 400 多篇中、短篇小说，10 多个剧本，创造了一种风格独特、言简意赅、艺术精湛的抒情心理小说。其代表作《变色龙》、《套中人》堪称俄国文学史上精湛而完美的艺术珍品，前者成为见风使舵、善于变相、投机钻营者的代名词；后者成为因循守旧、畏首畏尾、害怕变革者的符号象征。

Leo Tolstoy

列夫·托尔斯泰（1828—1910），俄国作家。他出身于俄国一个贵族家庭，父母双亡，由亲戚抚养成人。早年生活放荡，后因厌倦自身状况，加入炮兵部队并开始文学创作生涯，耗时六年写出伟大的小说《战争与和平》，反映了他自身的双重性格。他创作的另一部俄国文学杰作《安娜·卡列尼娜》以一曲悲歌预示了作者本身的一场道德与精神危机，这种危机在《忏悔》、《我的信仰》等作品中达到顶峰。其主要作品还有长篇小说《复活》和悲剧性短篇小说《哈吉·穆拉特》。他最终自缚于可以说是基督教无政府主义的思想之中。

Customary use of artifice is the sign of a small mind, and it always happens that he who uses it to cover one spot uncovers himself in another.

La Rochefoucauld, French writer

习惯做假是小人的特点,但常常是某人做假遮住了一个污点,但却在另一处露了马脚。

——拉罗什福科,法国作家

Procrastination is the grave in which opportunity is buried.

Anonymous

拖延是埋没机遇的坟墓。

——佚名

A man that studied revenge keeps his own wounds green.

Francis Bacon, British essayist and philosopher

念念不忘复仇的人,自己的伤口永远也不会愈合。

——培根,英国散文作家、哲学家

Men blush less for their crimes than for their weaknesses and vanity.

Jean de La Bruyere, French moralist

人更多的时候是为其软弱和虚荣,而不是为其罪恶脸红。

——拉布吕耶尔,法国伦理学家

What the world needs is some "do give a damn" pills.

William Meninger, American psychoanalyst

这个世界所需要的是一些"请认真一点儿"的药丸。

——门尼格,美国心理分析学者

Without civic morality communities perish; without personal morality their survival has no value.

Bertrand Russell, British philosopher

没有公德,社会不复存在;没有个人德行,个人的存在也失去价值。

——罗素,英国哲学家

Revenge is dangerous: it may hurt you as well as your enemy.

Aesop, Ancient Greek fable writer

报复是危险的:它会伤害敌人,也会伤害自己。

——伊索,古希腊寓言作家

Virtue is a kind of health, beauty, and good habit of the soul.

Plato, Ancient Greek philosopher

美德是一种心灵的健康、美丽和好习惯。

——柏拉图,古希腊哲学家

Assume a virtue, if you have it not.

William Shakespeare, British dramatist

如果你没有好的品行,就假装。

——莎士比亚,英国剧作家

If you only help people because you can get something out of it for yourself, you'll be disappointed.

Aesop, Ancient Greek fable writer

如果你只是为了得到什么东西而帮助别人,那你就会失望。

——伊索,古希腊寓言作家

Judge not, that we be not judged.

Holy Bible

你不接受评判,就不要评判别人。

——《圣经》

Even in the best, most friendly and simplest relations of life, praise and commendation are essential, just as grease is necessary to wheels that they may run smoothly.

Leo Tolstoy, Russian writer

就是在最好的、最友善的、最淳朴的人际关系中,赞美和表扬也是需要的,就像轮子需要上油,以便使它转动起来。

——列夫·托尔斯泰,俄国作家

No honest man can argue both sides well.

Sophocles, Ancient Greek dramatist

没有一个诚实的人能够两面讨好。

——索福克勒斯,古希腊剧作家

Patience is the best remedy for every trouble.

Plautus, Ancient Roman dramatist

忍耐是解决一切麻烦的最佳办法。

——普拉图斯,古罗马剧作家

He who is in adversity would have succour; Let him be generous while he rests secure.

Sadi, Iranian poet

谁想在困难时得到帮助,就应在平日里宽以待人。

——萨迪,伊朗诗人

No one can stop the wind. It must go where it is sent, but it will not hurt those who are not proud.

Aesop, Ancient Greek fable writer

没有人能够挡住风的,它来去自由,周而复始,不过它决不会伤害那些谦逊的人。

——伊索,古希腊寓言作家

The ones who love others will always be loved by others and the ones who respect others will always be respected by others.

Mencius, Ancient Chinese philosopher,

爱人者,人恒爱之;敬人者,人恒敬之。

——孟子,中国古代哲学家

No one believes a liar—even when he tells the truth.

Aesop, Ancient Greek fable writer

谁也不相信爱撒谎的人说的话——哪怕他说的是真话。

——伊索,古希腊寓言作家

Patriotism itself is a necessary link in the golden chains of our affections and virtues.

Coleridge, British poet

爱国主义本身是爱和美德组成的金链上必不可少的一环。

——柯尔律治,英国诗人

We need to restore the full meaning of that old word, duty. It is the other side of rights.

Pearl Buck, American female writer

我们必须恢复“责任”这个古老之词的完整含义,这是权利的另一面。

——赛珍珠,美国女作家

Minds are conquered not by arms, but by love and magnanimity.

Benedict de Spinoza, Dutch philosopher

征服思想不可依赖武力,而须凭借爱和宽容。

——斯宾诺莎,荷兰哲学家

Charms strike the sight, but merits win the soul.

Alexander Pope, British poet

美貌吸引目光,美德赢得心灵。

——蒲柏,英国诗人

Meet success like a gentleman and disaster like a man.

Fredrich Edwin Birkenhead, British statesman and lawyer

谦逊地面对成功,勇敢地面对挫折。

——伯肯黑德,英国政治家、律师

Genius is one per cent inspiration and ninety-nine per cent perspiration.

Thomas Edison, American inventor

天才是百分之一的灵感加上百分之九十九的汗水。

——爱迪生,美国发明家

Giving yourself your word to do something ought to be no less sacred than giving your word to others.

André Gide, French writer

向自己保证要完成一件事,如同向别人许诺一样神圣。

——纪德,法国作家

Love is more than money, and a kind word will give more pleasure than a present.

Sir John Lubbock, British naturalist

爱比金钱更重要,良言比礼物能带来更多的快乐。

——卢伯克爵士,英国博物学家

Personality is to man what perfume is to a flower.

Schwab, American businessman

品质之于人,犹如芳香之于鲜花。

——施瓦布,美国实业家

The measure of a man's real character is what he would do if he knew he would never be found out.

Thomas Macaulay, British historian

衡量一个人真正的品质,要看他在知道永远也不会被人发现的情况下做些什么。

——麦考利,英国历史学家

Virtue is bold, and goodness never fearful.

William Shakespeare, British dramatist and poet

美德是勇敢的,善良从来无所畏惧。

——莎士比亚,英国剧作家、诗人

An optimist sees an opportunity in every calamity; a pessimist sees a calamity in every opportunity.

Winston Churchill, British statesman

乐观者从每一次灾难中看到机遇,悲观者从每一次机遇中看到灾难。

——丘吉尔,英国政治家

Patience: n. A minor form of despair, disguised as a virtue.

Ambrose Bierce, American journalist and writer

耐心:名词,一种轻微的绝望,通常都装扮成一种美德。

——安布罗斯·比尔斯,美国记者、作家

Delay always breeds danger and to protract a great design is often to ruin it.

Cervantes, Spanish writer

拖延孕育危险,耽搁一项重大的计划无异于毁灭它。

——塞万提斯,西班牙作家

The inappropriate cannot be beautiful.

Frank Lloyd Wright, American architect

合适得体才会美。

——赖特,美国建筑师

Praise is like sunlight to the human spirit, we cannot flower and grow without it.

Graham Green, British writer

对人的精神来说,赞扬就像阳光一样,没有它我们便不能开花生长。

——格林,英国作家

Ambrose Bierce

比尔斯（1842—?），美国新闻记者、作家。他生于俄亥俄州，曾参加南北战争，后成为记者，往来于美国和英国之间，著有多部讽刺性幽默故事集，如《魔鬼的喜悦》、《在人生中期》和《魔鬼辞典》(*The Devil's Dictionary*, 1906）等。他一生愤世嫉俗，后在墨西哥失踪。

Frank Lloyd Wright

赖特（1867—1959），美国建筑师。他生于威斯康星州，土木工程学专业毕业，以设计低层草原风格住宅闻名，他是宽敞空间式设计领域的创新者，被公认为在设计中将现代私人住宅与周围自然环境完美结合的最重要的设计师。其重要作品有东京帝国饭店和纽约市古根海姆艺术博物馆等。

赖特设计的流水别墅

Friedrich Schiller

席勒（1759—1805），德国诗人、剧作家。他出生于内卡河畔的马尔巴赫，先学法律后学医，18 岁时写出第一部成名作《强盗》，引起强烈反响。其作品《欢乐颂》后被贝多芬谱成《第九合唱交响曲》。从 1794 年起，他与歌德开始长达 10 年的密切合作并硕果累累。其代表作有《华伦斯坦》三部曲、《奥尔良的姑娘》和《威廉·退尔》等。创作力旺盛的他，还写诗、翻译、排戏等。席勒的主要剧作已有中译本，《阴谋与爱情》等已多次被搬上中国舞台。

Theodore Roosevelt

西奥多·罗斯福（1858—1919），美国共和党政治家、第 26 届总统（1901—1909）。他生于纽约，就读于哈佛大学，1898 年招募一支志愿骑兵部队（罗斯福莽骑兵）参加古巴战争，回国后任纽约州长。1900 年他当选为美国副总统，麦金利遇刺身亡后继任总统，1904 年连任，因调停俄日战争获 1906 年诺贝尔和平奖。他是一名扩张主义者，主张建立强大海军，提出反托拉斯和反垄断法案，为社会改革实行“公平交易”政策。

There is, however, a limit at which forbearance ceases to be a virtue.

Edmund Burke, British statesman

克制有限度,超过了限度就不再是美德。

——伯克,英国政治家

Plain living and high thinking.

William Wordsworth, British poet

生活要朴素,情操要高尚。

——华兹华斯,英国诗人

A brave man risks his life, but not his conscience.

Friedrich Schiller, German dramatist and poet

勇敢的人可用生命冒险,但不以良心冒险。

——席勒,德国剧作家、诗人

Optimism is a good characteristic, but if carried to an excess it becomes foolishness.

Theodore Roosevelt, American President

乐观是种优秀品质,但过分乐观就是愚蠢了。

——西奥多·罗斯福,美国总统

Initiative is doing the right thing without being told.

Elbert Hubbard, American writer

主动性是指在没人告诉的情况下做正确的事情。

——哈伯德,美国作家

What you do not want done to yourself, do not do to others.

Confucius, Ancient Chinese philosopher and educator

己所不欲,勿施于人。

——孔子,中国古代哲学家、教育家

You are indeed charitable when you give, and while giving, turn your face away so that you may not see the shyness of the receiver.

Kahlil Gibran, Lebanese poet and novelist

当你施舍时,你的确慈悲为怀,不过当你施舍时,请转过脸去,不要看接受者的羞惭。

——纪伯伦,黎巴嫩诗人、小说家

A man should never be ashamed to own that he has been in the wrong, which is but saying, in other words, that he is wiser today than he was yesterday.

Alexander Pope, British poet

人不应该为承认自已的错误而感到惭愧,因为这就等于在间接地说他今天比昨天更聪明了。

——蒲柏,英国诗人

Try not to become a man of success but rather to become a man of value.

A. Einstein, American scientist

不要将目标定为成功,要为做一个有价值的人努力。

——爱因斯坦,美国科学家

Laziness is like a lock, which bolts you out of the storehouse of information and makes you an intellectual starveling.

Bernard Shaw, British dramatist

懒惰就像一把锁,锁住了知识的仓库,使你的智力匮乏。

——萧伯纳,英国剧作家

It is not enough to do good thing; one must do it by the right way.

John Morley, British statesman

人不仅要做好事,更要以正确的方式做好事。

——约翰·莫利,英国政治家

Morality is not really the doctrine of how to make ourselves happy but of how we are to be worthy of happiness.

Immanuel Kant, German philosopher

道德不是真正指导人们如何使自己幸福的信条,而是指导人们如何值得享有幸福的学说。

——康德,德国哲学家

Nothing is easier than to deceive one's self.

Demosthenes, Ancient Greek orator

再没有什么比欺骗自己更容易的了。

——狄摩西尼,古希腊演说家

The greater the man, the more restrained his anger.

Ovid, Ancient Roman poet

人越伟大,越能克制怒火。

——奥维德,古罗马诗人

All men are liable to error; and most men are, in many points, by passion or interest, under temptation to it.

John Locke, British philosopher

人都会犯错误。大多数人常常由于欲望或兴趣的诱惑而犯错误。

——洛克,英国哲学家

The ultimate measure of a man is not where he stands in moments of comfort, but where he stands at times of challenge and controversy.

Martin Luther King, American civil-rights leader

一个人的价值并不体现在他享乐的时候,而是面对挑战和困境的时刻。

——马丁·路德·金,美国民权运动领导人

Be willing to have it so. Acceptance of what has happened is the first step to overcoming the consequence of any misfortune.

William James,
American philosopher and psychologist

愿意承认现实,接受已发生的事,是克服不幸事件后果的第一步。

——威廉·詹姆斯,美国哲学家、心理学家

I can see, and that is why I can be so happy in what you call the dark, but which to me is golden.

Helen Keller, American writer

我可以看见,这就是为什么在你所说的黑暗中我能这样快乐。你称其为黑暗,在我看来则是金色。

——海伦·凯勒,美国作家

Never bend your head. Always hold it high. Look the world straight in the eye.

Helen Keller, American writer

永远不要低下你的头,永远高昂着头,勇敢地正视这个世界。

——海伦·凯勒,美国作家

Mental will is a muscle that needs exercise, just like muscles of the body.

Lynn Jennings,
American distance runner

正如身体的肌肉一样,意志力也需要磨炼。

——琳·詹宁斯,美国长跑运动员

I would prefer even to fail with honour than win by cheating.

Sophocles, Ancient Greek dramatist

我宁愿光荣地失败,也不愿以欺骗获胜。

——索福克勒斯,古希腊剧作家

Character is what you are in the dark.

D. L. Moody, American religious leader

暗处最能反映一个人的真正品格。

——穆迪,美国宗教领袖

Sometimes, we are proud of what is of little use to us, and forget to be thankful for the things that are our real help and strength.

Aesop, Ancient Greek fable writer

有时,对我们来讲几乎没有多大用处的东西我们会引以为荣,反而忘记了感激那些能给予我们真正帮助和力量的东西。

——伊索,古希腊寓言作家

How much more grievous are the consequences of anger than the causes of it.

Marcus Aurelius, Ancient Roman Emperor

生气的后果比生气的原因更严重。

——马可·奥勒利乌斯,古罗马皇帝

To be anger is to revenge the faults of others upon ourselves.

Alexander Pope, British poet

生气是因别人的错误而惩罚自己。

——蒲柏,英国诗人

The drop of rain makes a hole in the stone, not by violence, but by falling.

Latimer

雨滴穿石,不是靠强力,而是靠持之以恒。

——拉蒂默

Action
行动

You never know what you can do till you try.

Frederick Marryat, British novelist

除非你亲自尝试一下,否则你永远不知道你能够做什么。

——马里亚特,英国小说家

Activity is the only road to knowledge.

George Bernard Shaw, British dramatist

行动是通往知识的唯一道路。

——萧伯纳,英国剧作家

Execute every act of thy life as though it were thy last.

Marcus Aurelius, Ancient Roman Emperor

做每一件事时都把它当作你生命中的最后一件事。

——马可·奥勒利乌斯,古罗马皇帝

Half of our mistakes in life arise from feeling where we ought to think, and thinking where we ought to feel.

John Chelten Colin

我们生命中一半的错误在于该深思熟虑时我们意气用事,而该凭感觉行事时又思前想后。

——约翰·切顿·科林

A thing that has not been begun cannot be finished.

Robert Henri, American painter

还没开始的工作不可能有完成之日。

——罗伯特·亨利,美国画家

For of all sad words of tongue or pen, the saddest are these: "It might have been!"

J. G. Whittier, American poet

口说或笔写的所有悲哀的词句中,最悲哀的是"本来有可能是这样的!"

—— 惠蒂埃,美国诗人

First, say to yourself what you would be; and then do what you have to do.

Epictetus, Ancient Roman philosopher

首先默默告诉自己想成为什么样的人,然后再着手必须做的事情。

——爱比克泰德,古罗马哲学家

People are always neglecting something they can do in trying to do something they can't do.

Edgar Watson Howe, American journalist

人们致力于力所不能及的事情的同时,往往忽略了力所能及的事情。

——埃德加·沃森·豪,美国记者

Resolve to perform what you ought. Perform without fail what you resolve.

Benjamin Franklin,

American statesman, writer, and scientist

自己该做的事下定决心去做;决心去做的事一定做好。

——本杰明·富兰克林,

美国政治家、作家、科学家

Great works are performed not by strength, but by perseverance.

Samuel Johnson, British writer and critic

完成伟大的事业不在于体力,而在于坚忍不拔的毅力。

——约翰逊,英国作家、评论家

Nothing is so exhausting as indecision, and nothing so futile.

Bertrand Russell, British philosopher

悬而不决最熬人、最无益。

——罗素,英国哲学家

Make up your mind to act decidedly and take the consequences. No good is ever done in this world by hesitation.

T. Huxley, British biologist

下定决心果断行动,并承担后果。在这世上犹豫不决成就不了任何事。

——赫胥黎,英国生物学家

The great end of life is not knowledge but action.

T. Huxley, British biologist

人生的伟大目的不在于知而在于行。

——赫胥黎，英国生物学家

Do all the good you can,
By all the means you can,
In all the ways you can,
In all the places you can,
At all the times you can,
To all the people you can,
As long as ever you can.

John Wesley, British religious leader

尽可能地做一切好事；
尽可能地采取一切手段；
尽可能地利用一切方式；
尽可能地利用一切地方；
尽可能地利用一切时间；
尽可能地惠及一切人；
尽可能地持之以恒。

——韦斯利，英国宗教领袖

I am a slow walker, but I never walk backwards.

Abraham Lincoln, American President

我走得很慢，但从不倒退。

——林肯，美国总统

Thomas Henry Huxley

赫胥黎（1825—1895），英国生物学家。他生于伦敦，在伦敦大学学医，曾任海军外科医师，在一次访问澳大利亚海岸时对自然史产生兴趣。1854 年，他就任皇家矿业学院自然史教授，成为一流的达尔文主义解释者，并在所著《人在自然界中的地位》一书中为达尔文主义增加了人类学的观点。他还研究化石，同时也写文章，用“不可知论”（他首先使用的学术名词）的观点论述了神学和哲学。

John Wesley

韦斯利（1703—1791），英国宗教领袖，福音派教士，循道宗创立者。他生于林肯郡，求学于牛津大学，1725 年起任牧师，逐渐成为诨名循道者的一个小团体的领袖——这个小团体后来推动了伟大的福音运动。他是一位多产作家，写有语法、历史著作、传记，出过赞美诗集、布道文和日记集，还办过杂志。

Abraham Lincoln

林肯（1809—1865），美国政治家，第 16 任总统（1861—1865），美国南北战争时期的北方领袖。1809 年，林肯出身于肯塔基州一个伐木工人的家庭，迫于生计，他先后干过店员、村邮务员和劈栅栏木条等多种工作。1834 年，他当选为伊利诺伊州议员，从此开始了他的政治生涯。当时，美国奴隶制猖獗，他明确地宣布了他要“为争取自由和废除奴隶制而斗争”的政治主张。1860 年，他当选为总统，并率领北方军队赢得了南北战争的胜利，废除了黑奴制度。1864 年，林肯再度当选为总统。但不幸的是，1865 年 4 月 14 日晚，他在华盛顿福特剧院观剧时突然遭到枪击，次日清晨与世长辞。

The smallest actual good is better than the most magnificent promises of impossibilities.

Rose MaCawlay, British femal writer

最微小的实际好处也比无法实现的最堂而皇之的许诺强。

——麦考莉,英国女作家

He is no wise man who will quit a certainty for an uncertainty.

Samuel Johnson, British writer

为没有把握的事而放弃有把握的事,绝不是聪明人。

——约翰逊,英国作家

Wisely and slow, the stumble that run fast.

William Shakespeare, British dramatist

凡事三思而行,跑得太快会摔倒。

——莎士比亚,英国剧作家

I don't wait for moods. You accomplish nothing if you do that. Your mind must know it has got down to work.

Pearl Buck, American female writer

我从不等待情绪的来临。如果你一味等待,就将一事无成。你必须牢记,只有动手才能有所得。

——赛珍珠,美国女作家

Action speaks louder than words.

Longfellow, American poet

行动胜于言语。

——郎费罗,美国诗人

All that you do, do with your might; things done by halves are never done right.

R. H. Stoddard, American poet

做一切事都应尽力而为,半途而废永远不行。

——斯达德,美国诗人

Deeds are fruits, words are but leaves.

Joseph Drake, American poet

行为才是果实,言语不过是树叶。

——德雷克,美国诗人

With talent, you do what you like. With genius, you do what you can.

Jean Ingres, French painter

有才能的人,做自己喜爱的事;有天赋的人,做自己能做的事。

——让·安格尔,法国画家

A man can do what he wants, but not want what he wants.

Albert Einstein, American scientist

一个人可以做他想做的一切,却不能要求得到他想要的一切。

——爱因斯坦,美国科学家

Do what you ought, and come what can.

George Herbert, British poet

做你该做的事,不要问结果怎样。

——赫伯特,英国诗人

Vision without action is merely a dream. Action without vision just passes the time. Vision with action can change the world!

Joel Arthur Barker,
American expert of management

没有行动的远见只是一个梦想。没有远见的行动仅随时间流逝。有行动的远见能改变世界!

——乔·亚瑟·巴克,美国管理专家

Nothing is more terrible than ignorance in action.

Erasmus, *Dutch humanist*

最可怕的事莫过于行动中的无知。

——伊拉斯谟,荷兰人文主义者

Our deeds determine us, much as we determine our deeds.

George Eliot, *British female writer*

干什么样的事决定了我们是什么样的人;同样,什么样的人便决定了干什么样的事。

——乔治·艾略特,英国女作家

Take time to deliberate; but when the time for action arrives, stop thinking and go in.

John Andrew, *American leader against slavery*

考虑时不要匆忙,但一旦行动的时刻来到,就要毫不犹豫地投身其中。

——安德鲁,美国废奴运动领导人

The more we do, the more we can do; the busier we are, the more leisure we have.

William Hazlitt, British critic and essayist

事做得越多越能干,人越忙越有空闲。

——黑兹利特,英国评论家、散文家

Action springs not from thought, but from a readiness for responsibility.

Dietrich Bonhoeffer, German theologian

行动并不来自思想,而是来自愿意承担责任。

——朋谔斐尔,德国神学家

Nothing will ever be attempted if all possible objections must be first overcome.

Samuel Johnson, British writer

如果做一件事之前需要驳倒所有的反对意见,那一件也做不成。

——塞缪尔·约翰逊,英国作家

Behind many acts that are thought ridiculous, there lie many wise and weighty motives.

La Rochefoucauld, French writer

在许多人认为可笑的行动背后有着许多重要而又富有智慧的动机。

——拉罗什富科,法国作家

Something attempted, something done.

Menander, Ancient Greek dramatist

有所尝试,有所成。

——米南德,古希腊剧作家

Time
时间

Yesterday is history. Tomorrow is a mystery and Today is a gift: that's why we call it "The Present".

Bryan Dyson,
President of the Coca-Cola Company

昨天已成历史,明天仍是未知,而今天是上帝的恩赐。正因如此,我们称今天为"礼物"。

——布莱恩·戴森,可口可乐公司总裁

Tomorrow I will live, the fool does say. Today itself is too late; the wise lived yesterday.

Marrial

明天我就真正生活,愚人总是这样说。其实今天就已经晚了,明智的人昨天就开始生活了。

——马利尔

Misspending a man's time is a kind of self-homicide.

Sir Charles Halifax, *British statesman*

虚度时光无异于自杀。

——哈利法克斯侯爵,英国政治家

To choose time is to save time.

Francis Bacon,
British essayist and philosopher

合理安排时间就是节约时间。

——培根,英国散文作家、哲学家

In the life of one man, never the same time returns.

Thomas Steams Eliot, British poet and critic

在人的一生中,同样的时光永不复回。

——托马斯·艾略特,英国诗人、评论家

Write it on your heart that every day is the best of the year.

Ralph Waldo Emerson, American thinker

铭记在心:每天都是一年中最好的日子。

——爱默生,美国思想家

Weep no more, no sigh, nor groan. Sorrow calls no time that's gone.

John Fletcher, British dramatist

别再哭泣,别叹息,别呻吟;悲伤唤不回流逝的时光。

——弗莱彻,英国剧作家

Time is a bird forever on the wing.

T. W. Robertson, British dramatist

时间是一只永远飞翔的鸟。

——罗伯逊,英国剧作家

Lost wealth may be replaced by industry, lost knowledge by study, lost health by temperance of medicine, but lost time is gone forever.

Samuel Smiles, British writer

失去的财富可以靠勤奋换来,失去的知识可以靠学习得来,失去的健康可以靠药物节制得来,但是失去的光阴一去不复返。

——斯迈尔斯,英国作家

Do you love life? Then do not squander time; for that's the stuff life is made of.

Benjamin Franklin,
American statesman, writer, and scientist

你热爱生命吗? 那么,别浪费时间,因为生命是由时间组成的。

——富兰克林,美国政治家、作家、科学家

Experience proves that most time is wasted, not in hours, but in minutes. A bucket with a small hole in the bottom gets just as empty as a bucket that is deliberately kicked over.

Paul Meyer, French linguist

经验证明,大部分时间都是被一分钟一分钟地而不是一小时一小时地浪费掉的。一只底部有个小洞的桶和一只故意踢翻的桶同样会空的。

——迈耶,法国语言学家

How much of human life is lost in waiting!

Ralph Waldo Emerson, American thinker

多少生命在等待中浪费。

——爱默生，美国思想家

No man is rich enough to buy back his past.

Oscar Wilde, British writer

再有钱的人也买不来时光倒流。

——王尔德，英国作家

The golden age is before us, not behind us.

Mark Twain, American writer

黄金时代在我们面前而不在我们背后。

——马克·吐温，美国作家

Know the true value of time: snatch, seize, and enjoy every moment of it. No idleness, no laziness, no procrastination; never put off till tomorrow what you can do today.

Chesterfield, British diplomat and writer

要知道时间的真正价值：抓住、留住并享受每一刻，不要懒散，不要怠惰，不要拖沓；千万不要把今天能做的事推到明天。

——切斯特菲尔德，英国外交家、作家

Voltaire

伏尔泰（1694—1778）是18世纪法国资产阶级启蒙运动的旗手，被誉为“思想之王”、“法兰西最优秀的诗人”。他出生于巴黎，早年攻读法律，后转而投身文学创作，曾因开罪于奥尔良公爵而被投入巴士底狱，在狱中将悲剧《俄狄浦斯王》修改完毕，该剧使他成名。他的主要著作有《哲学书简》、《哲学辞典》，讽刺性短篇小说《老实人》等。他的思想对导致法国大革命的知识界思潮的形成有着重大影响。

William Shakespeare

莎士比亚（1564—1616），英国著名戏剧家和诗人，欧洲文艺复兴时期人文主义文学的集大成者。他出生于沃里克郡一个富裕市民家庭，曾在当地文法学校学习。他13岁时家道中落辍学经商，约1586年前往伦敦。他先在剧院门前为贵族顾客看马，后逐渐成为剧院的杂役、演员、剧作家和股东。1616年，莎士比亚由于生病离开了人世。在这52年的生涯中，他为世人留下了37个剧本，一卷14行诗和两部叙事长诗。其主要作品有《罗密欧与朱丽叶》，四大悲剧《哈姆雷特》、《奥赛罗》、《李尔王》和《麦克白》，历史剧《理查三世》、《亨利三世》，喜剧《仲夏夜之梦》、《第十二夜》、《皆大欢喜》等。莎士比亚的作品既与当时所属的环境密切相连，也超越时空，反映了人类共通的特质。他的喜剧热闹喧哗，悲剧真挚无奈，而对白中流露出对生命的观察，直指人性的清明与软弱，使他的作品成为人类不朽的文学瑰宝。

The time of life is short; to spend that shortness basely, it would be too long.

William Shakespeare, British dramatist

人生苦短,若虚度年华,则短暂的人生就太长了。

——莎士比亚,英国剧作家

There is nothing longer than time, for it is inexhausted, and nothing shorter than it, for our plans can not be fulfilled in time.

Voltaire, French thinker

最长的莫过于时间,因为它永无穷尽;最短的也莫过于时间,因为我们所有的计划都来不及完成。

——伏尔泰,法国思想家

What we love to do we find time to do.

John Spalding, American educator and writer

喜欢做就能找到时间去做。

——斯波尔丁,美国教育家、作家

The Net is a waste of time, and that's exactly what's right about it.

William Gibson, American writer

网络浪费时间,并且这恰是它权力所在。

——吉布森,美国作家

Courage
勇气

People do not lack strength；they lack will.

Victor Hugo，*French writer*

人们缺少的不是力量，而是勇气。

——雨果，法国作家

He who loses wealth loses much；he who loses a friend loses more；but he who loses courage loses all.

Cervantes，*Spanish writer*

失去财产的人损失很大，失去朋友的人损失更多，而失去勇气的人则失去了一切。

——塞万提斯，西班牙作家

If you're knocked down，you can't lose your guts. You need to play with supreme confidence or else you'll lose again，and then losing becomes a habit.

Joe Paterno，*American football coach*

如果你被打败了，你千万不要失去勇气，你需要以最大的信心继续努力，否则你就会再次失败，然后失败就会成为一种习惯。

——乔·帕泰诺，著名美式足球教练

Don't give up. Don't lose hope. Don't sell out.

Christopher Reeve, American actor

不要放弃,不要丢掉希望,不要屈服。

——克里斯托夫·里夫,美国演员

One isn't necessarily born with courage, but one is born with potential. Without courage, we cannot practice any other virtue with consistency. We can't be kind, true, merciful, generous or honest.

Maya Angelou, American female writer

一个人并不一定天生勇敢,但一定有与生俱来的勇敢的潜质。没有勇气,我们不可能持之以恒地实践其他美德,不可能真,不可能善,不可能仁慈、慷慨和诚实。

——玛亚·安吉拉,美国女作家

Whatever is not nailed down is mine; whatever I can pry loose is not nailed down.

Collis P. Huntington, American businessman

凡是没有确定的,都是我的;凡我还有机会争取的,都是没有确定的。

——亨廷顿,美国实业家

Courage is the basic virtue for everyone so long as he continues to grow, to move ahead.

Rollo May, American psychologist

勇气是每个人首要的美德,只要他还在成长,还在前进。

——罗洛·梅,美国心理学家

Samuel Johnson

约翰逊（1709—1784），人称约翰逊博士，辞书编纂家、评论家和诗人。他生于斯塔福德郡，出身于书商家庭，就读于牛津大学，后做过教师、记者。从1747年起，他用八年时间编纂了《英语辞典》，并编辑道学主义期刊《漫谈者》，逐渐成为文学评论的权威人士和社会名流。他还著有诗集《诗人传》，并编辑出版莎士比亚作品集。

Marie Curie

居里夫人（1867—1934），法国籍波兰科学家。她生于波兰华沙，与法国丈夫皮埃尔·居里一起在巴黎大学研究磁和放射现象，并发现了镭。皮埃尔和玛丽·居里及贝克勒耳因发现放射现象而共获1903年诺贝尔物理学奖。丈夫死后，居里夫人接任其教授职位，1910年分离出钋和镭，获1911年诺贝尔化学奖。她死于白血病，很可能是因长期受放射线照射所致。在世界科学史上，玛丽·居里是一个永远不朽的名字。这位伟大的女科学家，以自己的勤奋和天赋，在物理学和化学领域，都作出了杰出的贡献，并因此成为唯一一位在两个不同学科领域、两次获得诺贝尔奖的著名科学家。作为杰出科学家，居里夫人有一般科学家所没有的社会影响，尤其因为是成功女性的先驱，她的典范激励了很多人。

We must believe that we are gifted for something, and that this thing, at what ever cost, must be attained!

Marie Courier, Polish scientist

我们必须相信,对于某些事我们是有天赋的才能的。无论付出何种代价,我们都要完成它。

——居里夫人,波兰科学家

There is nothing which human courage will not undertake, and little that human patience will not endure.

Samuel Johnson, British writer

人的勇气能承担一切重负;人的耐心能忍受绝大部分痛苦。

——塞缪尔·约翰逊,英国作家

我喜欢的名人名言

Some of my favorite quotes that are not contained in this book are:

我喜欢的名人名言

Some of my favorite quotes that are not contained in this book are:

Culture Nourishes the Mind

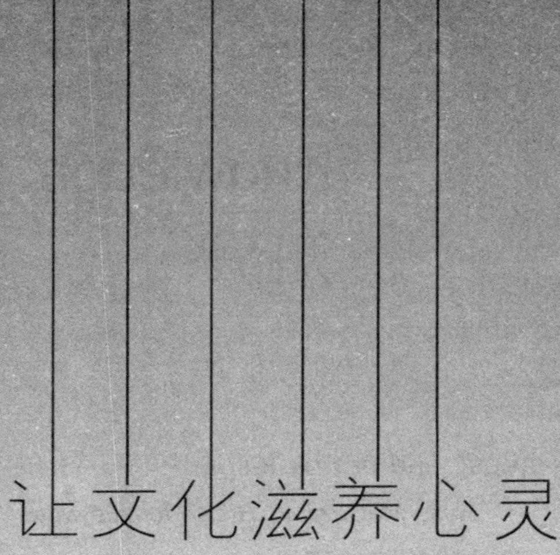

让文化滋养心灵

美的东西是永恒的喜悦。

A thing of beauty is a joy forever.

Knowledge
知识

Knowledge advances by steps, and not by leaps.

Rose MaCawlay, British female writer

知识的增长并非一蹴而就，而是靠长期的积累。

——麦考莉，英国女作家

Knowledge of languages is the gateway to wisdom.

Francis Bacon, British essayist and philosopher

语言知识是通往智慧的道路。

——培根，英国散文作家、哲学家

Nothing is so good for an ignorant man as silence, and if he knew this he would no longer be ignorant.

Sadi, Iranian poet

对于无知的人最好的事情莫过于沉默。倘若他知道这一点，他也就不再无知了。

——萨迪，伊朗诗人

Knowledge is power.

Francis Bacon, British essayist and philosopher

知识就是力量。

——培根，英国散文作家、哲学家

A free man obtains knowledge from many sources besides books.

Thomas Jefferson, American President

一个自由的人除了从书本上获取知识外,还可以从许多别的渠道获得知识。

——杰斐逊,美国总统

A great part of the information I have was acquired by looking up something and finding something else on the way.

Adas Franklin, American humorist

我的大部分知识都是这样获得的:在寻找某些东西时意外地发现了另外的东西。

——A. 富兰克林,美国幽默作家

It is the peculiarity of knowledge that those who really thirst for it always get it.

Richard Jeffries, British naturalist

真正渴求知识者总能得到它,这就是知识的特性。

——杰弗里斯,英国博物学家

Knowledge is a comfortable and necessary retreat and shelter for us in an advanced age; and if we do not plant it when young, it will give us no shade when we grow old.

Chesterfield, British diplomat and writer

知识使我们老年时能舒适地隐退,并有所寄托;如果年轻时不学习知识,年老时我们就不能受益。

——切斯特菲尔德,英国外交家、作家

Aristotle

亚里士多德（公元前384—公元前322年），古希腊最伟大的思想家、哲学家和教育家。他出生于希腊殖民地的色雷斯，是柏拉图的学生，亚历山大大帝的老师，他的成就大大超过了他的老师，著述几乎涉及当时人类知识的每一个领域，可以说是古希腊集大成的思想家。他总结了泰勒斯以来古希腊哲学发展的结果，首次将哲学和其他科学区别开来，开创了逻辑学、伦理学、政治学和生物学等学科的独立研究。他的学术思想对西方文化、科学的发展产生了巨大的影响。

Socrates

苏格拉底（公元前469—公元前399年），著名的古希腊唯心主义哲学家、教育家，与他的学生柏拉图及柏拉图的学生亚里士多德并称为“希腊三贤”。他出生于伯里克利统治的雅典黄金时期，死于雅典的败落时期，早年生活不详。他主张有知识的人才具有美德，才能治理国家。能把人的先天就有的、潜在的知识和美德诱发出来的，这就是教育。他还首先发明和使用了以师生共同谈话、共商问题、获得知识为特征的问答式教学法。苏格拉底无论是生前还是死后，都有一大批狂热的崇拜者和一大批激烈的反对者。他一生没留下任何著作，他的品德和学说不朽地保留在柏拉图的对话录中，对西方哲学产生了不可估量的影响。

Plato

柏拉图（公元前427—公元前347年），古希腊最著名的唯心主义哲学家、伦理学家和政治家。他出身于雅典贵族家庭，是古希腊哲学家苏格拉底的学生。柏拉图一生著作甚多，其主要作品有《理想国》和《法律论》。

The larger the island of knowledge, the longer the shoreline of wonder.

Ralph Sockman, American religious leader

知识之岛愈大,未知的海岸线愈长。

——索克曼,美国宗教领袖

There is always one good, that is knowledge; there is only one evil, that is ignorance.

Socrates, Ancient Greek philosopher

善只有一个,那就是知识;恶只有一个,那就是愚昧。

——苏格拉底,古希腊哲学家

All men naturally desire to know.

Aristotle, Ancient Greek philosopher

求知是人的天性。

——亚里士多德,古希腊哲学家

Knowledge which is acquired under compulsion obtains no hold on the mind.

Plato, Ancient Greek philosopher

强灌的知识记不牢。

——柏拉图,古希腊哲学家

Knowledge is a treasure, but practice is the key to it.

Thomas Fuller, British clergyman and historian

知识是一座宝库,而实践是开启宝库的钥匙。

——富勒,英国牧师、历史学家

Love is ever the beginning of knowledge as fire is of light.

Thomas Carlyle, British historian and essayist

知识总是从爱好开始,犹如光总是从火开始一样。

——卡莱尔,英国历史学家、散文家

Discussion is an exchange of knowledge, argument in life is an exchange of ignorance.

Robert Quillen,
American humorist, journalist, and cartoonist

讨论是交流知识,争论是交换无知。

——罗伯特·奎林,
美国幽默作家、记者、卡通画家

The desire of knowledge, like the thirst of riches, increases ever with the acquisition of it.

Laurence Sterne, Irish novelist

对知识的渴望就像对财富的欲望一样,越是拥有,越想增加。

——斯特恩,爱尔兰小说家

Poverty of speech is the outward evidence of poverty of mind.

Bruce Barton, American businessman

说话内容贫乏是心智贫乏的表现。

——巴顿,美国实业家

It is easy to learn something about everything, but difficult to learn everything about anything.

Emmons

对每件事知道一些是容易的,对任何一件事详细知道是困难的。

——艾蒙斯

Education
教育

Education is a progressive discovery of our own ignorance.

W. Durant, American historian and essayist

教育是一个逐步发现自己无知的过程。

——杜兰特,美国历史学家、散文家

From the very beginning of his education, the child should experience the joy of discovery.

A. N. Whitehead,
British mathematician and philosopher

在儿童教育的初始阶段,应让他体会到发现的快乐。

——怀特海,英国数学家、哲学家

Education is the ability to listen to almost anything without losing your temper or self-confidence.

Robert Frost, American poet

教育能使人具备听到任何话都不动怒或丧失自信的能力。

——弗罗斯特,美国诗人

The desire of appearing clever often prevents us becoming so.

La Rochefoucauld, French writer

想显示聪明反而常常妨碍我们变聪明。

——拉罗什福科,法国作家

The language of the lips is easily taught, but who can teach the language of the heart?

Mohatma Gandhi, Indian statesman

口头的语言是容易教的,但是谁能教心灵的语言呢?

——圣雄甘地,印度政治家

The purpose of education is to replace an empty mind with an open one.

Malcolm Forbes, American publisher

教育的目的是用能接受新思想的头脑去取代一个空虚的灵魂。

——福布斯,美国出版商

It is strange that all great men should have some little grain of madness mingled with whatever genius they possess.

Moliere, French writer

很奇怪,大凡伟人在他们所拥有的天分中都混杂着一些疯狂的成分。

——莫里哀,法国作家

Better be unborn than untaught, for ignorance is the root of misfortune.

Plato, Ancient Greek philosopher

与其不受教育,不如不生,因为无知是不幸的根源。

——柏拉图,古希腊哲学家

Alfred Nobel

诺贝尔（1833—1896），瑞典化学家，黄色炸药的发明者和诺贝尔奖的创立者。他生于瑞典斯德哥尔摩，发明了雷管引爆、无烟火药等。他还参与建立了一个工业帝国，制造了许多他发明的产品，积聚了大量的财富。根据他的遗嘱，以其遗产的大部分作为基金设立了“诺贝尔奖金”，他为人类的和平与进步作了最后的努力。诺贝尔奖首次颁发于1901年，分别授予在物理学、化学、生理学或医学、文学与和平事业中对人类作出最大贡献的人（第六项经济学奖是为纪念他而在1969年增设的）。

The roots of education are bitter, but the fruit is sweet.

Aristotle, Ancient Greek philosopher

教育的根是苦的,但果实是甜的。

——亚里士多德,古希腊哲学家

The direction in which education starts a man will determine his future life.

Plato, Ancient Greek philosopher

启蒙教育的方向将决定一个人的未来生活。

——柏拉图,古希腊哲学家

The aim of the college, for the individual student, is to eliminate the need in his life for the college; the task is to help him become a self-educating man.

Charles Wright Mills, American sociologist

对于学生个人来说,大学的目的在于使他在以后的生活中摆脱对学校的需要,学校的任务在于帮助他成为能够进行自我教育的人。

——米尔斯,美国社会学家

To spread knowledge is to spread happiness.

Alfred Nobel, Swedish chemist

传播知识就是播种幸福。

——诺贝尔,瑞典化学家

If you think education is expensive, try ignorance.

Derek Bok,

American educator, President of Harvard University

如果你觉得教育昂贵,那你试试无知。

——德里克·博克,

美国教育家、哈佛大学校长

We receive three educations, one from our parents, one from our schoolmaster, and one from the world. The third contradicts all that the first two teach us.

Montesquieu, French philosopher and jurist

我们接受三种教育:一种来自父母,一种来自学校,另一种来自社会。第三种教育同前两种矛盾。

——孟德斯鸠,法国哲学家和法理学家

A man who has never gone to school may steal from a freight car, but if he has had a university education, he may steal from the whole railroad.

Theodore Roosevelt, American President

一个没有上过学的人可能会从一节货车上偷东西,但如果他受过高等教育,他有可能从整个铁路上偷东西。

——西奥多·罗斯福,美国总统

Esthetic education is the cultivation of souls, a higher interest in life out of the appreciation of beautiful things. This appreciation makes people understand a higher realm of life beyond money and material substances without indulging in material desires and fussing about narrow gratitude or grief and small gains and losses.

Romain Rolland, French writer

美育是一种心灵的陶冶，是由于对美好事物的欣赏而得到的高格调的生活情趣。这种欣赏可以使人了解在金钱和物质之外的、更高的人生境界，不致沉迷于物欲，也不致斤斤计较狭小的恩怨得失。

——罗曼·罗兰，法国作家

Learning
学习

To learn is a natural pleasure, not confined to philosophers, but common to all men.

Aristotle, Ancient Greek philosopher

学习是一种自然的快乐,这并不限于哲学家,而是对所有的人都一样。

——亚里士多德,古希腊哲学家

The more I read, the more I meditate; and the more I acquire, the more I am enabled to affirm that I know nothing.

Voltaire, French thinker

我读的越多,思考越深入;收获越大,越使我确信自己浅薄无知。

——伏尔泰,法国思想家

If we would have new knowledge, we must get a whole world of new questions.

Susan Lange,
American female symbolism aestheticsist

要获得知识,必须提出大量问题。

——苏珊·朗格,美国女性符号论美学家

Everyone complains of his memory, but no one complains of his judgement.

La Rochefoucauld, *French writer*

人人报怨自己的记忆力,却无人报怨自己的判断力。

——拉罗什福科,法国作家

If you don't learn to think when you are young, you may never learn.

Thomas Edison, *American inventor*

如果年轻时不学会思考,那就永远学不会思考。

——爱迪生,美国发明家

In a world as empirical as ours, a youngster who does not know what he is good at will not be sure what he is good for.

Edgar Friedenberg, *British educator*

在我们这个经验的世界里,一个不懂得自己精通什么的青年不会确切地知道他的价值所在。

——埃德加·弗里登伯格,英国教育家

If you have great talents, industry will improve them; if you have but moderate abilities, industry will supply their deficiency.

Joshuas Reynolds, *American female essayist*

如果你很有天赋,勤勉会使其更加完善;如果你能力一般,勤勉会补足其缺陷。

——雷诺兹,美国女散文家

Just as eating against one's will is injurious to health, so study without a liking for spoils the memory, and it retains nothing it takes in.

Leonardo da Vinci, Italian artist and painter

正如被逼进食于健康不利,学习若无兴趣,不仅有损记忆而且一无所获。

——达·芬奇,意大利艺术家、画家

It is not enough to have a good mind. The main thing is to use it well.

René Descartes,
French mathematician and philosopher

仅仅有好的头脑还不够,重要的是要善于使用它。

——笛卡儿,法国数学家、哲学家

If I have seen further than most men, it is by standing on the shoulders of giants.

Isaac Newton, British scientist

如果我比大多数人看得远些,那只是因为我是站在巨人的肩膀上。

——牛顿,英国科学家

Youth is the time to study wisdom; old age is the time to practice it.

Rousseau, French thinker

青年是学习智慧之季,老年是实践智慧之时。

——卢梭,法国思想家

Leonardo da Vinci

达·芬奇（1452—1519），意大利画家、艺术家。他生于佛罗伦萨，受过初等教育，后学习雕塑与绘画。其代表作有《最后的晚餐》、《蒙娜丽莎》、《岩下圣母》等。在他的艺术风格上，他几乎没有受到古代艺术家的影响，他的实践建立在对大自然的研究上。他很难单独说成是一位画家、建筑师、音乐家、工程师或雕塑家，他有着广博的知识，对许多学科有深刻的理解，对生物学、解剖学、生理学、流体力学、机械及航空学都有独到见解，远远超出了他所处的那个时代。

René Descartes

笛卡儿（1596—1650），法国数学家、唯理论哲学家。他生于法国拉阿伊，他认为“我思，故我在”，人的心灵和肉体是相互独立的，这种二元论使得人类的自由和不朽成为可能。他的著作有《形而上学的沉思》、《方法谈》等。他建立了解析几何学，并为光学的发展做出了重要贡献。

Isaac Newton

牛顿（1642—1727），西方科学史上最具影响力的科学家。他出生于英国林肯郡。他的功绩在于为现代物理科学的塑造提供了基础的智力手段。牛顿发现了三条最基本的运动定律和万有引力定律。基于这些规律，地球上所有的物理现象都变得可以预测、井然有序、合乎理性，并可用技术加以操控。只是到了20世纪，当科学家们开始研究最小的粒子——原子的性质时，牛顿定律的有效性才开始被质疑。

Cultivation to the mind is as necessary as food for the body.

Cicero, Ancient Roman statesman and orator

学习对于头脑如同食物对于身体,不可缺少。

——西塞罗,古罗马政治家、演说家

He who nothing questions, nothing learns.

Stephen Gosson, British writer

什么也不问的人,什么也学不到。

——戈桑,英国作家

The three foundations of learning: seeing much, suffering much, and studying much.

Willa Catherall, American writer

求学的三个基本条件:多观察、多磨砺、多研究。

——卡塞罗尔,美国作家

If you're not confused, you're not paying attention.

Tom Peters, American expert of management

如果你不感到困惑,说明你并没有集中精力。

——彼得斯,美国管理专家

Teachers open the door, but you must enter by yourself.

Anonymous

师傅领进门,修行在个人。

——佚名

Histories make men wise; poems witty; the mathematics subtle; natural philosophy deep; moral grave; logic and rhetoric able to contend.

Francis Bacon, British essayist and philosopher

历史使人明智;诗词使人灵秀;数学使人周密;自然哲学使人深刻;伦理使人庄重;逻辑修辞学使人善辩。

——培根,英国散文作家、哲学家

You can learn from everyone.

Derek Boke, President of Harvard University

你可以向任何人学习。

——博克,美国哈佛大学校长

You will never have what you like until you learn to like what you have.

Goethe, German writer

在学会喜欢你已有的东西以前,你永远不会得到你喜欢的东西。

——歌德,德国作家

Experience is the father of wisdom and memory is the mother.

Claude Bernard, French physiologist

经验是智慧之父,记忆是智慧之母。

——贝尔纳,法国生理学家

I have learned silence from the talkative, toleration from the intolerant, and kindness from the unkind; yet strange, I am ungrateful to those teachers.

Kahlil Gibran, Lebanese poet and novelist

我从健谈者那里学会了沉默,从不容异己者那里学会了宽容,从心地不善者那里学会了善良;但奇怪的是,我不感激这些老师。

——纪伯伦,黎巴嫩诗人、小说家

The true art of memory is the art of attention.

Samuel Johnson, British writer

记忆的真谛就是专心。

——塞缪尔·约翰逊,英国作家

Reading
阅读

We live in an age that reads too much to be wise.

Oscar Wilde, British writer

我们生活在一个读书太多以至于把自己读傻了的年代。

——王尔德，英国作家

A man may as well expect to grow stronger by always eating as wiser by always reading.

David Collier,
American Professor of political science

要想更加强壮就要吃好；要想更加睿智就要阅读。

——大卫·科利尔，美国政治学教授

There is more treasure in books than in all the pirate's loot on *Treasure Island*, and best of all, you can enjoy these riches every day of your life.

Walt Disney,
American businessman and producer

书中的财宝多于《金银岛》中海盗的财产，而且最重要的是你可以在生命中的每一天享受这些财宝。

——沃尔特·迪斯尼，
美国实业家、电影制片人

Francis Bacon

培根（1561—1626），英国文艺复兴时期最重要的散文作家、哲学家。他不但在文学、哲学上多有建树，在自然科学领域里，也取得了重大成就。他出生于英国伦敦，求学于剑桥大学和格雷律师学院，相继任律师、检察官、大法官。他的哲学思想充分反映在其著作《学术的进展》和《新工具》中。他强调的归纳方法对科学研究起到了重大的促进作用。他的《培根随笔集》富含哲理，读者甚多。

Montesquieu

孟德斯鸠（1689—1755），法国哲学家和法学家。他生于法国波尔多附近的布雷德堡，就读于波尔多大学，后成为一名律师，但以后转而投身于科学研究和文学创作。1726 年，他定居巴黎，随后用了几年时间广泛游历，研究政治和社会制度。其最著名的作品是对法律和政治问题进行比较研究的《论法的精神》，对 18 世纪的欧洲产生了巨大的影响。

William Somerset Maugham

毛姆（1874—1965），英国著名的小说家和戏剧家。他出身于律师家庭，曾在伦敦情报部门工作，战后周游世界各地。他一生共创作了长篇小说 4 部、短篇小说 150 多篇、剧本 30 多部。不过，毛姆本人对自己的评价却很谦虚："我只不过是二流作家中排在前面的一个。"作为奥斯卡·王尔德风化案之后的一代英国作家，毛姆在自己的作品中小心地避免了与同性恋有关的各种题材，尽管他本人也曾拥有一段长达三十年的同性恋情。其代表作有《月亮和六便士》、《人性枷锁》和《寻欢作乐》等。

To acquire the habit of reading is to construct for yourself a refuge from almost all the miseries of life.

William Somerset Maugham, British novelist

养成读书的习惯，就给你自己建造了一座逃避人生几乎所有不幸的避难所。

——毛姆，英国小说家

Like reading is to exchange the periods of loneliness unavoidable in life for the periods of delight.

Montesquieu, French philosopher and jurist

爱读书，就是以人生无法回避的寂寞时光，换取美妙的时光。

——孟德斯鸠，法国哲学家、法理学家

Some books are to be tasted, others to be swallowed, and some few to be chewed and digested.

Francis Bacon,
British essayist and philosopher

一些书可以浅尝辄止，一些书可以狼吞虎咽，而有些书则需要细嚼慢咽，好好消化。

——培根，英国散文作家、哲学家

Read, mark, learn, and inwardly digest.

The Book of Common Prayer

读、标记、学习，然后内部消化。

——《英国国教祈祷书》

No book is really worth reading at the age of ten which is not equally, and often far more, worth reading at the age of fifty and beyond.

C. S. Lewis, British scholar and writer

真正值得在 10 岁时阅读的书,也值得或更值得在 50 岁甚至于 50 岁以后阅读。

——路易斯,英国学者、作家

Reading makes a full man, meditation a profound man, discourse a clear man.

Benjamin Franklin,
American statesman, writer, and scientist

阅读培养学问丰富的人,思考培养见识深刻的人,演讲培养思路清晰的人。

——本杰明·富兰克林,
美国政治家、作家、科学家

A classic is something that everyone wants to have read and nobody wants to read.

Mark Twain, American writer

经典作品是人人都不想读,但人人都希望自己已经读过的书。

——马克·吐温,美国作家

I suggest that the only books that influence us are those for which we are ready, and which have gone a little farther down our particular path than we have gone ourselves.

E. M. Forster, British writer

我认为能够影响我们的是那些我们有能力理解,并由在我们前进的路上比我们走得远的先行者所写的书。

——福斯特,英国作家

Reading without thinking will not lead to gains, and even if there is a slight impression, it will not take root and most of it will soon be forgotten.

Arthur Schopenhauer, German philosopher

读书而不加以思考,决不会有心得,即使稍有印象,也浅薄而不生根,大部分很快被遗忘。

——叔本华,德国哲学家

Innovation
创新

All good things which exist are the fruits of originality.

John Stuart Mill, British economist

一切美好的事物都是创新的结果。

——米尔,英国经济学家

Everyone is necessarily the hero of his own life story.

John Barth, American novelist

人人都应该是自己生活的主角。

——约翰·巴思,美国小说家

Everything that is really great and inspiring is created by the individual who can labor in freedom.

Albert Einstein, American scientist

自由无拘、努力奋斗的人创造一切真正伟大而激动人心的事件。

——爱因斯坦,美国科学家

All that we are is the result of what we have thought. The mind is everything. What we think, we become.

Buddha

我们的全部存在是我们思想的结果,心智就是一切。我们会成为我们想成为的人。

——佛陀

Don't undermine your worth by comparing yourself to others. It is because we are different that each of us is special.

Bryan Dyson,

President of the Coca-Cola Company

不要盲目与他人比较,而低估自身的价值。须知,人与人之间有差异,才显出个性。

——布莱恩·戴森,

可口可乐公司总裁

Follow your own course, and let people talk.

Alighieri Dante, Italian poet

走自己的路,让别人去说吧。

——但丁,意大利诗人

Too many people are thinking of security instead of opportunity. They seem more afraid of life than death.

James Byrnes, American statesman

太多太多的人一直考虑的是安全而不是机会,看来他们怕活着胜于怕死。

——拜内斯,美国政治家

Nobody is bored when he is trying to make something that is beautiful, or to discover something that is true.

William Inge, American dramatist

当一个人试图创造美的事物或者发现真理时,他从不感到厌烦。

——威廉·英奇,美国剧作家

Don't believe everything you hear.

Aesop, Ancient Greek fable writer

别听到什么就相信什么。

——伊索,古希腊寓言作家

Think for yourself. What everyone else is doing may not be the right thing.

Aesop, Ancient Greek fable writer

要独立思考。别人做的事不一定是对的。

——伊索,古希腊寓言作家

No one knows what he can do till he tries.

Publilius Syrus, Latin writer of proverbs

一个人只有经过尝试才知道自己能做什么。

——普布里利亚斯·西拉斯,拉丁语格言作家

Man's greatness lies in his power of thought.

Blaise Pascal, French scientist

人的伟大之处在于其思想的力量。

——帕斯卡,法国科学家

Thinking always ahead, thinking always of trying to do more, brings a state of mind in which nothing seems impossible.

Henry Ford, American manufacturer

不断地思考未来,不断地尝试着多做事,会达到一种无所不能的精神状态。

——亨利·福特,美国制造商

Blaise Pascal

帕斯卡（1623—1662），法国数学家、物理学家。他生于法国克莱蒙费朗。自幼聪明好学，对数学、物理尤其感兴趣。他12岁就学完了欧几里德几何，16岁时发表了一篇有关圆锥曲线的出色论文，从此正式踏进了法国学术界的大门，潜心研究，一发而不可收。他发现了大气压强随着高度变化的规律；建立了流体的帕斯卡定律，为流体静力学的建立奠定了基础。1647年，他发明了一种计算装置，后又发明了气压计、水压机和注射器，1654年以前一直在巴黎进行数学研究和从事社会活动。他只活了39岁就英年早逝。人们为了纪念他，用他的名字命名压强的国际单位制单位，简称“帕”，国际符号为Pa。

Henry Ford

亨利·福特（1863—1947），美国汽车工程师、实业家。他生于美国密歇根州，1893年首次制造出汽油发动机汽车，1903年创办福特汽车公司，首次采用现代的“装配线”成批生产技术，生产出著名的T型汽车。

New opinions are always suspected, and usually opposed, without any other reason but because they are not already common.

John Locke, British philosopher

新观点总是受到怀疑,往往还遭到反对,这只不过是因为它还未为人所共知。

——洛克,英国哲学家

Creativity is no more teachable than heritable. No more than the most detail-perfect doll can transubstantiate into a living, breathing baby.

Norma Rosen, American novelist

创造能力既不是遗传的,也不是教得会的。正如再怎样完美制作的洋娃娃,也不能够变成一个会呼吸的活的婴儿。

——罗森,美国小说家

Nature's mighty law is change.

Robert Burns, British poet

自然界的强大法则就是变。

——彭斯,英国诗人

We cannot change anything unless we accept it.

Carl Jung, Swiss psychiatrist

对一件事情我们必须先接受它,才能改变它。

——荣格,瑞士精神病学家

Growth and change are the law of all life. Yesterday's answers are inadequate for today's problems—just as the solutions of today will not fill the needs of tomorrow.

Franklin Roosevelt, American President

成长与变化是一切生命的规律。昨日的答案不适用于今日的问题,正如今天的方法不能满足明天的需求。

——富兰克林·罗斯福,美国总统

The reasonable man adapts himself to the world; the unreasonable man persists in trying to adapt the world to himself. Therefore, all progress depends on the unreasonable man.

George Bernard Shaw, British dramatist

理性的人使自己适应世界,非理性的人坚持要世界适应自己,所以一切进步得靠非理性的人。

——萧伯纳,英国剧作家

Only those who will risk going too far can possibly find out how far one can go.

Thomas Steams Eliot, British poet and critic

只有那些敢冒险走远路的人,才能知道自己究竟能走多远。

——托马斯·艾略特,英国诗人、评论家

There is nothing permanent except change.

Heracleitus, Ancient Greek philosopher

唯有变化才是永恒的。

——赫拉克利特,古希腊哲学家

Discontent is the first step in the progress of a man or a nation.

Oscar Wilde, British writer

不满足是一个人或一个国家发展的第一步。

——王尔德,英国作家

Dare and the world always yields. If it beats you sometimes, dare it again and again and it will succumb.

W. M. Thackeray, British novelist

大胆挑战,世界总会让步。如果有时候你被它打败了,不断地挑战,它总会屈服的。

——萨克雷,英国小说家

Anything one man can imagine, other men can make real.

Jules Verne, French science fiction writer

但凡人能想象到的事物,必定有人能将它实现。

——儒勒·凡尔纳,法国科幻作家

In order to be irreplaceable, one must always be different.

Coco Chanel, French designer

一个人要想不被别人取代,就得有与众不同之处。

——夏奈尔,法国服装设计师

Originality does not consist in saying what no one has ever said before, but is saying exactly what you think.

J. F. Stephen, British jurist

新意不在于说出别人从未说过的话,而是要说出你自己的想法。

——史蒂芬,英国法理学家

Coco Chanel

夏奈尔（1883—1971），法国女时装设计师。她生于法国索米尔，1912年以前设计女帽，第一次世界大战后在巴黎开设了一家女装店，20世纪20年代她给妇女时装带来了一场革命。她设计上的许多特色，如服装上的人造珠宝饰物和晚会上用的围巾至今仍很流行。她于1938年退休，但1954年又返回时装界并取得了意想不到的成功，使“Chanel”成为国际女装及化妆品著名品牌。

Jules Verne

儒勒·凡尔纳（1828—1905），法国作家。他生于法国西部海港南特，自幼热爱海洋，向往远航探险。18岁时，他遵父嘱，去巴黎攻读法律，可是却爱上了文学和戏剧。后来，凡尔纳与大仲马合作创作了剧本《折断的麦秆》并得以上演，这标志着凡尔纳在文学界取得了初步的成功。凡尔纳创作出《气球上的五星期》后，在16家出版社遭到冷遇，他愤然将书稿投入火中，被妻子抢救出来，送入第17家出版社后被出版。《气球上的五星期》出版之后，凡尔纳的创作进入了一个多方面的探索时期，写出了《地心游记》、《从地球到月球》、《环绕月球》、《海底两万里》、《神秘岛》、《80天环游地球》、《太阳系历险记》、《两年假期》等一系列优秀作品。

Albert Einstein

爱因斯坦（1879—1955），美国科学家。他出生于德国乌耳姆，小时候沉默寡言，甚至被认为非常笨，17岁进入苏黎世工业大学，开始对物理学进行研究。他的科学工作成为20世纪物理学的奠基石。他的狭义和广义相对论为我们理解自然界的基本规律以及空间、质量和能量的概念提供了新的依据。1934年，他出版的文选《我理解的世界》和《晚年集》被一再重印，这些文选包含了科学的本质、社会主义、黑人与白人的关系、犹太复国主义及道德的腐朽等不同话题，对19世纪自由主义的明智见解直到今天仍然值得一读。他于1921年获诺贝尔物理学奖。

Archimedes

阿基米德（约公元前287—公元前212年），希腊数学家。他生于叙拉古，可能到过埃及，并在亚历山大求学。普遍认为，他因建造对付罗马人的攻城器械、建造现在仍用于提升水的“阿基米德螺旋泵”，以及发现物体的浮力原理时所发出的“我发现它了”的呼喊而受人缅怀。然而，他对数学真正重大的贡献在于他发现了可用于求出球体、圆柱体、抛物面体及其他平面图形的面积和体积公式。他创立了流体静力学，他的天文学著作已失传。罗马人攻陷叙拉古时，他因沉浸于数学演算而未理会一个罗马士兵的查问口令，不幸被杀。

Science

科学

Science without religion is lame, religion without science is blind.

Albert Einstein, American scientist

没有宗教的科学是瘸子,没有科学的宗教是瞎子。

——爱因斯坦,美国科学家

When a man sits with a pretty girl for an hour, it seems like a minute. But let him sit on a hot stove for a minute—and it's longer than an hour. That's relativity.

Albert Einstein, American scientist

当一个男人和一个漂亮的女孩坐在一起时,一小时就像一分钟;但如果让他坐在火炉上,一分钟比一小时还长。这就是相对论。

——爱因斯坦,美国科学家

Give me a lever long enough and a fulcrum on which to place it, and I shall move the Earth.

Archimedes, Greek physicist

给我一根足够长的杠杆和一个支点,我就能撬动地球。

——阿基米德,希腊物理学家

There is no royal road to science, and only those who do not dread the fatiguing climb of gaining it numinous summits.

Karl Marx, German revolutionary

在科学上没有平坦的大道,只有不畏艰辛沿着其崎岖之路攀登的人,才有希望达到它光辉的顶点。

——马克思,德国革命家

Science is organized knowledge. Wisdom is organized life.

Kant, German philosopher

科学是有组织的知识,智慧是有组织的生活。

——康德,德国哲学家

The brotherly spirit of science, which unites into one family all its votaries of whatever grade, and however widely dispersed throughout the different quarters of the globe.

Franklin Roosevelt, American President

科学的博爱精神把分散在世界各地、各种热心科学的人联结成一个大家庭。

——富兰克林·罗斯福,美国总统

True science teaches, above all, to doubt and be ignorant.

De Unamuno, Spanish philosopher

真正的科学首要的是教人去怀疑,并让人感到自身的无知。

——乌纳穆诺,西班牙哲学家

Every great advance in science has issued from a new audacity of the imagination.

John Dewey, American educator

科学的每一次重大进步都源于一个大胆而新奇的想象。

——杜威,美国教育家

Wisdom entered not into a malicious mind, and science without conscience is but the ruin of soul.

Francois Rabelais, French writer

恶毒的心灵不长智慧,没有良知的科学只能毁灭心灵。

——拉伯雷,法国作家

Culture
文化

If there were no cultural wealth—knowledge, literature, art, music as well as the beauty displayed in different forms, life would become dim, narrow, as to lose the true happiness of man.

Sukhomlinski,
Union of Soviet Socialist Republics educator

如果没有文化财富——知识、文学、艺术、音乐以及各种形式表现出来的美，那么生活就会变得暗淡、狭隘，从而失去了人生真正的幸福。

——苏霍姆林斯基，前苏联教育家

Culture, the acquainting ourselves with the best that has been known and said in the world, and thus with the history of the human spirit.

Matthew Arnold, *British poet and literary critic*

文化令我们知悉世界上最好的知识和话语，从而了解人类精神的历史。

——马修·阿诺德，英国诗人、文学评论家

Without art, the crudeness of reality would make the world unbearable.

George Bernard Shaw, British dramatist

如果没有艺术,现实的粗俗将使这个世界不堪忍受。

——萧伯纳,英国剧作家

Our sweetest songs are those that tell of saddest thought.

Percy Bysshe Shelley, British poet

我们最美妙的歌是那些讲述最悲伤思想的歌。

——雪莱,英国诗人

Music is the art of thinking with sounds.

Jules Combarie

音乐是用声音思想的艺术。

——柯柏瑞

A great poem is a fountain forever overflowing with the waters of wisdom and delight.

P. B. Shelley, British poet

伟大的诗篇是永远喷出智慧和欢欣之水的喷泉。

——雪莱,英国诗人

A novel is a mirror walking along a main road.

Stendhcl, French writer

一部小说犹如一面在大街上行走的镜子。

——司汤达,法国作家

A picture is a poem without words.

Horace Mann, American educator

一幅图画是一首没有文字的诗。

——贺拉斯·曼，美国教育家

Art is I; science is we.

Claude Bernard, French physiologist

艺术需要个性；科学需要合作。

——贝尔纳，法国生理学家

Art is uncompromising, and life is full of compromises.

Gunter Grass, German novelist

艺术是不妥协的；而生活充满了妥协。

——冈特·格拉斯，德国小说家

For art to exist, for any sort of aesthetic activity or perception to exist, a certain physiological precondition is indispensable: intoxication.

Friedrich Nietzsche, German philosopher

有种生理状况对艺术的产生，对任何美学活动或体验都是不可缺少的，这就是欣喜陶醉。

——尼采，德国哲学家

I paint objects as I think them, not as I see them.

Pablo Picasso, Spanish painter

我的作品是思想而非视觉的产物。

——毕加索，西班牙画家

Gunter Grass

格拉斯（1927—　），德国小说家。他生于德国但泽，求学于杜塞尔多夫艺术学院和柏林国立美术学院，在二战中服兵役，成为战俘。他的第一部小说《铁皮鼓》使他成为当今最伟大的德国小说家。由于小说中对纳粹生动而真实的描写，在德国引起轰动。他的作品包含着渊博的知识和丰富的阅历，不断向现状提出挑战，对过去的认识提出质疑。他的重要作品有《猫和鼠》、《非人的岁月》、《局部的麻醉》和《比目鱼》等。他于1999年获诺贝尔文学奖。

Pablo Picasso

毕加索（1881—1973），西班牙画家。他出身于一个美术教师家庭，从小随父习画，14岁进入巴黎巴塞罗那美术学校，两年后转入马德里深造。1898年，他的作品《阿拉贡的习俗》获金质奖章，此时他还是传统的艺术大师。但他不久开始发展自己的风格，创作了《亚威农的少女们》，成为第一次充分展示分析立体主义的范例。他的主要作品巨幅油画《格尔尼卡》用综合立体主义表现了西班牙内战中战争给人类带来的恐惧。他92岁高龄时在法国穆甘逝世。毕加索是20世纪早期艺术界举足轻重的人物，但他首先是一位伟大的创新者。

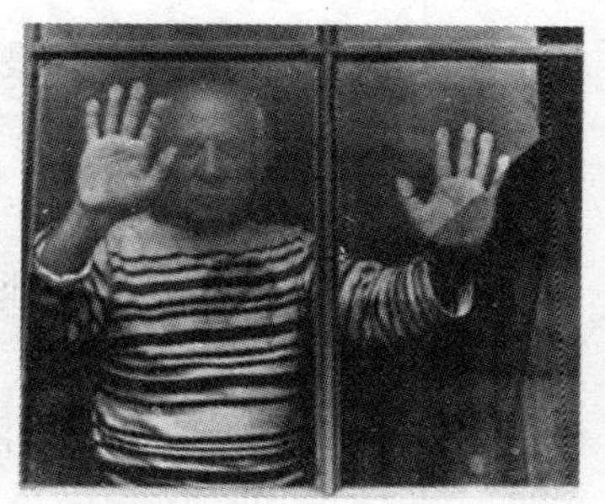

It took me fifteen years to discover I had no talent for writing, but I couldn't give it up because by that time I was too famous.

Robert Benchley, American humorist

我用了15年才发现我没有写作才能，但我无法放弃写作，因为那时我已太出名了。

——罗伯特·本奇利，美国幽默作家

It is as easy to dream a book as it is hard to write one.

Honoré de Balzac, French writer

梦想写一部书的轻松程度和实际写一部书的困难程度是一样的。

——巴尔扎克，法国作家

Poetry: the best words in the best order.

Samuel Taylor Coleridge, British poet

诗歌：最美文字的最佳排列。

——柯尔律治，英国诗人

A thing of beauty is a joy forever.

John Keats, British poet

美的东西是永恒的喜悦。

——济慈，英国诗人

Thinking is the talking of the soul with itself.

Plato, Ancient Greek philosopher

思想是灵魂在同自我交谈。

——柏拉图，古希腊哲学家

The most beautiful things are those that madness prompts and reason writes.

André Gide, French writer

最漂亮的作品是疯狂的激情和理性的创作相结合的产物。

——纪德,法国作家

Every work of art adheres to some system of morality. But if it be really a work of art, it must contain the essential criticism of the morality to which it adheres.

D. H. Lawrence, British writer

任何艺术作品都遵循一定的道德体系,但同时,任何真正的艺术作品都含有对它所遵循的道德体系的实质性的批判。

——劳伦斯,英国作家

Fill your paper with the breathings of your heart.

William Wordsworth, British poet

用心灵的呼吸填满你的文章。

——华兹华斯,英国诗人

Writing is a solitary occupation. Family, friends, and society are the natural enemies of the writer. He must be alone, uninterrupted, and slightly savage if he is to sustain and complete an undertaking.

Jessamyn West, American female writer

写作是孤独的职业,家庭、朋友和社会是作家的天敌。如果他想坚持并完成这个事业,他必须独自一人,不受干扰,甚至有点野蛮。

——杰丝敏·韦斯特,美国女作家

Learn to foster an ardent imagination; so shall you descry beauty which others passed unheeded.

Norman Douglas, British poet

学会培养富有激情的想象,如此你将发现别人忽视而错过的美。

——诺曼·道格拉斯,英国诗人

Such is beauty ever, neither in Rome nor in Athens, but whenever there is a soul to admire.

H. D. Thoreau, American writer and thinker

美既不在罗马也不在雅典,而是深藏于每颗欣赏美的心灵,这才是永恒的美。

——梭罗,美国作家、思想家

My way of joking is telling the truth; that is the funniest joke in the world.

George Bernard Shaw, British dramatist

我开玩笑的方法是实话实说,这就是世上最有意思的笑话。

——萧伯纳,英国剧作家

Deliver me from writers who say the way they live doesn't matter, I'm not sure a bad person can write a good book, if art doesn't make us better, then what on earth is it for.

Alice Walker, American female writer

对那些认为自己的生活方式无关紧要的作家,让我远离他们。我怀疑一个坏人能否写出好的作品。如果艺术不能使我们向善,那它有什么用。

——艾丽丝·沃克,美国女作家

George Bernard Shaw

萧伯纳（1856—1950），英国剧作家。他出身于爱尔兰都柏林一公务员家庭，1876年，移居伦敦，为报刊撰写音乐和戏剧评论，1885年，开始戏剧创作。其主要作品有剧本《圣女贞德》、《鳏夫的房产》、《华伦夫人的职业》、《人与超人》、《巴巴拉少校》和《皮格马利翁》等。他的剧作关注社会问题，语言活泼生动，人物形象鲜明，情节曲折，对世界戏剧事业有很大的影响。他于1925年获诺贝尔文学奖。

Alice Walker

艾丽斯·沃克（1944— ），美国女作家。她生于佐治亚州，求学于亚特兰大斯佩尔曼学院及劳伦斯学院，曾当过社会工作者、教师。她是一位才华横溢的诗人，同时又以小说闻名遐迩，如《紫色》（获普利策奖）。她还写有多部短篇小说集和散文集，包括《好女永不屈服》、《寻找母亲的花园》、《怀有快乐的秘密》等。

Auguste Rodin

罗丹（1840—1917），法国雕塑家。他出生于巴黎，早年学绘画，后拜雕塑家 A. L. 巴里为师。1875 年意大利之行，米开朗琪罗的作品使他大开眼界，从此摆脱了学院派的表现模式，确立了自己的创作方法。最重要的作品是为巴黎艺术博物馆所做的浮雕，这个包括 186 个人体，分别表现青春、恋情和地狱生活悲惨与痛苦的作品，耗去了他 37 年的时间，其中《思想者》、《乌戈利诺和他的儿子们》、《吻》、《永恒的偶像》等成为永远的经典。另一件重要作品《加莱义民》为他赢得了世界声誉。他还为雨果、巴尔扎克等做过胸像和纪念碑，作品均具有浪漫主义和现实主义的特点。其雕塑手法和构思，丰富了雕塑艺术的表现领域，对欧洲现代雕塑的发展产生了不可低估的影响。罗丹的作品曾于 1993 年在中国的北京、上海展出。

罗丹作品

Literature is a luxury; fiction is a necessity.

G. K. Chesterton, British writer and critic

文学是奢侈品,小说是必需品。

——切斯特顿,英国作家、评论家

The reality is more excellent than the report.

Emerson, American thinker

现实比报告更精彩。

——爱默生,美国思想家

All man are creative, but few are artists.

Paul Goodman,
American artist and social reformer

所有的人都有创造力,但成为艺术家的人寥寥无几。

——保罗·古德曼,美国艺术家、社会改革家

All music jars when the soul's out of tune.

Cervantes, Spanish writer

当内心失去和谐时,所有的音乐都刺耳。

——塞万提斯,西班牙作家

Beauty exists everywhere. To our eyes, it is not lack beauty but lack discovery.

Auguste Rodin, French sculptor

美是到处都有的。对于我们的眼睛,不是缺少美,而是缺少发现。

——罗丹,法国雕塑家

Humor has been well defined as thinking in fun while feeling in earnest.

Mark Twain, American novelist

幽默被人正确地解释为“以诚挚表达感受,寓深思于嬉笑”。

——马克·吐温,美国小说家

A true poet does not bother to be poetical. Nor does a nursery gardener scent his roses.

Jean Cocteau,
French poet, dramatist, and director

园丁不会在玫瑰花上喷洒香水,真正的诗人不会刻意表现诗意。

——让·科克托,法国诗人、剧作家、导演

Use simple language, short words and brief sentences. That is the way to write English—it is modern way and the best way.

Mark Twain, American writer

使用简单朴实的语言,小词和短句。这就是写英语的方式——现代的和最好的方式。

——马克·吐温,美国作家

Jean Cocteau

让·科克托（1889—1963），法国作家，超现实主义成员。他出身于巴黎附近拉斐特府的一个富有家庭，小时候就接触电影、戏剧。10岁那年，身为律师和业余画家的父亲自杀，成了他一生都无法摆脱的魔咒，悲剧主题在他日后的创作中循环出现。科克托少年时认识了普鲁斯特，“我所有的一切都来自于童年”，科克托用这句话来解释他不同寻常的一生。

他是20世纪的艺术全才，几乎涉足了所有现代艺术的创作领域。他不但作为诗人、戏剧家、小说家、批评家、雕刻家、画家、设计师、音乐策划人、电影制片人、导演和演员均成就斐然，而且还对现代艺术不断进行实验。关于他历来争议不断：波德莱尔式贵族公子的生活、鸦片、双性恋、巴黎风尚、天分、敏感、优雅、机智，19世纪的颓废气息与20世纪的叛逆在他身上融为一体。他还是《达·芬奇密码》一书中披露的秘密宗教组织郇山隐修会的大师。多才多艺的科克托被誉为“巴黎才子”，1955年入选为法兰西学院院士。

我喜欢的名人名言

Some of my favorite quotes that are not contained in this book are:

我喜欢的名人名言

Some of my favorite quotes that are not contained in this book are:

Home–life

在家

我们爱自己的家，

我们的脚可以离它而去，

可我们的心却不能。

We love our home,

though our feet can leave it,

yet our hearts cannot.

Health

健康

Health and intellect are the two blessings of life.

Menander, Ancient Greek dramatist

健康和才智是生活的两大幸福。

——米南德,古希腊剧作家

Grace is to the body what clear thinking is to the mind.

La Rochefoucauld, French writer

动作优雅同肢体的关系正如思想清晰同大脑的关系。

——拉罗什富科,法国作家

Some people allow one bad experience to affect their whole lives.

Aesop, Ancient Greek fable writer

有些人让一次不好的经历影响了自己的一生。

——伊索,古希腊寓言作家

Got health, the most important thing, more than success, more than money, more than power.

Mario Puzo, American writer

身体健康是最重要的事情,比成功、金钱、权力都重要。

——马里奥·普佐,美国作家

A light heart lives long.

William Shakespeare, British dramatist

豁达者长寿。

——莎士比亚,英国剧作家

Bowling is good for the bone and kidney; shooting for the lungs and breast; gentle walking for the stomach; riding for the head; and the like.

Francis Bacon, British essayist and philosopher

保龄球有助于强腰壮肾,射箭有助于舒胸扩肺,散步有益于肠胃,骑马有益于头颅,运动各有益处。

——培根,英国散文家、哲学家

Early to bed and early to rise, makes a man healthy, wealthy and wise .

Benjamin Franklin,
American statesman, writer, and scientist

早睡早起会使人健康、富有和聪明。

——富兰克林,美国政治家、作家、科学家

Sloth, like rust, consumes faster than labor wears.

Benjamin Franklin,
American statesman, writer, and scientist

懒惰像生锈一样,比操劳更能消耗身体。

——富兰克林,美国政治家、作家、科学家

The first wealth is health.

Ralph Waldo Emerson, American thinker

健康是人生第一财富。

——爱默生,美国思想家

Fitness is not only one of the most important keys to a healthy body; it is the basis of dynamic and creative intellectual activity.

John F. Kennedy, American President

身体的健美不仅是身体健康的关键因素之一,还是富有活力与创造性的智力活动的基础。

——约翰·肯尼迪,美国总统

The future is just old age and illness and pain…I must have peace and health. This is the only way.

James Whale, American director

未来不过是年老、疾病和痛苦……我一定要拥有平和与健康,这是唯一的方式。

——惠尔,美国电影导演

Rest is a good thing, but boredom is its brother.

Voltaire, French thinker

休息是件好事情,无聊却伴随而来。

——伏尔泰,法国思想家

Travel, in the younger sort, is a part of education; in the elder, a part of experience.

Francis Bacon, British essayist and philosopher

旅游对年轻人来说是一种教育,对老年人来说是一种经验。

——培根,英国散文作家、哲学家

Only those who keep interested in outside things and objects can keep healthy in spirit.

Bertrand Russell, British philosopher

唯有对外界事物抱有兴趣,才能保持人们精神上的健康。

——罗素,英国哲学家

Regular physical exercise not only develops the beauty of body and the harmony of movements, but also helps the formation of character and the training of will.

Sukhomlinski,

Union of Soviet Socialist Republics educator

经常进行体育锻炼,不仅能发展身体的美和动作的和谐,而且有助于良好性格的形成,锻炼意志力。

——苏霍姆林斯基,前苏联教育家

Health is certainly more valuable than money, because it is by health that money is procured.

Samuel Johnson, British writer

健康当然比金钱更宝贵,因为我们所赖以获得金钱的,就是健康。

——塞缪尔·约翰逊,英国作家

Growing
成长

Real beauty comes from learning, growing, and loving in the way of life. That is the Art of Life.

Anonymous

真正的美丽源于生命中不断地学习、成长和关爱。这就是生命的艺术。

——佚名

Never do today what you can do tomorrow. Something may occur to make you regret your premature action.

Aaron Burr, American statesman

不要在今天做你明天才能做的事,不成熟的行为会有令你后悔的事情发生。

——阿龙·布尔,美国政治家

Sometimes we are so concerned about giving our children what we never had growing up; we neglect to give them what we did have growing up.

James Dobson,
American, founder and host of Focus on the Family

有时候我们急于给孩子们提供我们成长时没有的东西,却忘了给他们我们成长时确实有过的东西。

——多布森,美国《关注家庭》创始人、拥有者

The only thing some people do is get older.

Edgar Watson Howe, American journalist

有些人唯一的变化就是变老。

——埃德加·沃森·豪,美国记者

The world is moving so fast these days that the man who says it can't be done is generally interrupted by someone doing it.

Elbert Hubbard, American writer

今天的世界发展得如此之快,以至于一个刚张口说某件事无法做的人往往就被正在做这件事的人打断。

——哈伯德,美国作家

As you grow older, you'll find the only things you regret are the things you didn't do.

Zachary Scott, American actor

随着年龄的增长,你将会发现,你懊悔的事常常是你过去没有做的事。

——斯科特,美国演员

I am not young enough to know everything.

Oscar Wilde, British writer

我不再年轻,不再无所不知。

——王尔德,英国作家

Geoffrey Chaucer

乔叟（约1343—1400），英国诗人。他生于伦敦，早期教育情况不详。他第一次被称为诗人是人们读到了他的《公爵夫人之书》以后，之后他创作了《百鸟议会》、《声誉之宫》、《贞女们的传说》以及收集在《坎特伯雷故事集》中的有关职员、法律界人士、修道院院长、修女及骑士等的故事。14世纪90年代，他创作了最著名的作品、未完成的《坎特伯雷故事集》。这部作品内容丰富，语言幽默、优美，充满了现实主义色彩，一直是英语叙事诗经典著作。乔叟死后葬于威斯敏特教堂，后人称之为“诗人之角”，莎士比亚、拜伦均葬于此处。他是英国第一位伟大的诗人，英国南部方言之所以被确立为英语书面语言，乔叟作品的影响是一个重要因素。

Katharine Hepburn

凯瑟琳·赫本（1907—2003），美国女演员。她生于康涅狄格州，在宾夕法尼亚州布林莫尔学院学习，1932年起在国际上以具有强烈个性的女演员而闻名。她演过许多有名的电影，《本年著名妇女》是她与男影星屈塞25年职业关系和个人情感的开始。她获得奥斯卡奖的影片有《牵牛花》、《猜猜谁来赴晚宴》、《冬天的狮子》和《金色池塘》，同时她也在舞台上演出戏剧和音乐剧，均获得巨大成功。

What the hell…you might be right; you might be wrong, but don't just avoid.

Katharine Hepburn, American actress

你既可能对,也可能错,这没关系,只要你不一味逃避。

——凯瑟琳·赫本,美国女演员

For time it is, age has great advantages; experience and wisdom come with age. Men may be old outrun, but not outwit.

Geoffrey Chaucer, British poet

因时间的规律,老年有老年的优势,经验和智慧与时俱进,人到老年可能体力不胜,但可以智胜。

——乔叟,英国诗人

If every day is an awakening, you will never grow old, you will just keep growing.

Gail Sheehy, American female writer and lecturer

如果每一天都是一次醒悟,你就不会变老,只会长大。

——盖尔·希伊,美国女作家、演讲家

Childhood
童年

Childhood is the most wonderful period in one's life; the child then is a flower, a fruit, dim intelligence, an endless activity and a burst of strong desire.

Honoré de Balzac, French writer

童年原是一生中最美妙的阶段,那时的孩子是一朵花,也是一颗果子,是一片朦朦胧胧的聪明,一种永不停息的活动,一股强烈的欲望。

——巴尔扎克,法国作家

The finest inheritance you can give to a child is to allow it to make its own way, completely on its own feet.

Isadora Duncan, American female dancer

你能留给孩子的最好财产莫过于允许他完全独立自主地摸索自己的道路。

——邓肯,美国舞蹈家

If you want your children to keep their feet on the ground, put some responsibility on their shoulders.

John Bryant, British essayist

若希望你的孩子脚踏实地,就让他们负些责任。

——布赖恩特,英国散文家

Isadora Duncan

伊莎多拉·邓肯（1877—1927），美国舞蹈家、编导、教师，现代舞的先驱，出生在美国加利福尼亚州。邓肯从小学习芭蕾，曾在欧洲各地演出，创立了与古典芭蕾相对立的自由舞蹈，主张把舞蹈建立在自然的节奏和动作之上。“最自由的身体蕴藏最高的智慧”是邓肯的艺术目标和准则。她因对婚姻和妇女解放不符合传统的看法而招致诽谤。1927 年，邓肯在法国因车祸逝世。她被誉为“现代舞之母”。

Charles Dickens

狄更斯（1812—1870），英国小说家。他生于汉普郡的兰波特，接受过一定的教育，22岁进入伦敦报界工作，为多家报刊写稿，同时发奋工作，写出数部成功的小说，这些作品创造了又一个莎士比亚式的人物，鞭挞了当时社会各种丑恶现象。他最早发表的小说是在一份月刊上连载的著名的《雾都孤儿》，此后相继发表了《匹克威克外传》、《老古玩店》、《大卫·科波菲尔》、《双城记》《远大前程》（曾译《孤星血泪》）等多部小说，并被改编为成功的影视作品。

Henry Wadsworth Longfellow

朗费罗（1807—1882），美国诗人。他生于缅因州波特兰，因具有翻译天才被送往欧洲学习，后受聘为哈佛大学现代语言和文学教授。他出版过多部作品，获巨大成功的是《歌谣及其他诗篇》，最受欢迎的作品是《海华沙之歌》，与众不同的是他运用了“印第安鼓”的韵律。

A torn jacket is soon mended; but hard words bruise the heart of a child.

H. W. Longfellow, American poet

一件破了的上衣很快能缝好,严厉的言辞却会伤害孩子的心灵。

——朗费罗,美国诗人

If there is anything that we wish to change the child, we should first examine it and see whether it is not something that could better be changed in ourselves.

Carl Jung, Swiss psychiatrist

假如我们想让孩子在某个方面有所改变,我们应首先检验一下,看看我们自己是否最好在这一方面变一变。

——荣格,瑞士精神病学家

In the little world in which children have their existence, whosoever brings them up, there is nothing so finely perceived and so finely felt, as injustice.

Charles Dickens, British writer

孩子们有他们自己的小天地,无论谁将他们抚养成人,都没有任何事情像不公正那样让他们如此细微地察觉和感受。

——狄更斯,英国作家

Children have more need of models than of critics.

Francis Bacon, British essayist and philosopher

比之批评,儿童更需要榜样。

——培根,英国散文作家、哲学家

Youth
青春

Youth is like spring, an over praised season.

Samuel Butler, British writer

青春像春天一样,是个被过分赞美的时期。

——塞缪尔·巴特勒,英国作家

I remember my youth and the feeling that will never come back any more, the feeling that I could last forever, outlast the sea, the earth, and all men.

Joseph Conrad, British novelist

我依然记得我的青春和已经一去不复返的青春感觉。那时,我觉得自己会长命百岁,即使海枯石烂也不会死亡。

——康拉德,英国小说家

Youth is not a time of life; it is a state of mind; it is not a matter of rosy cheeks, red lips and supple knees; it is a matter of the will, a quality of the imagination, a vigor of the emotions; it is the freshness of the deep spring of life.

Samuel Erman, American writer

青春不是人生中的一段光阴,它是一种精神状态。青春不是粉红的面颊、鲜艳的嘴唇、柔软的膝盖,而是深沉的意志、恢弘的想象、炽热的情感。青春是生命的深泉在涌流。

——俄尔曼,美国作家

Joseph Conrad

康拉德（1857—1924），英国小说家。他生于乌克兰，父母都是波兰人，1886年加入英国商船队成为英国公民，曾远涉重洋到过世界各地。他的第一部长篇小说是《阿尔马耶的蠢事》，他最著名的作品有《水仙号上的黑家伙》、《吉姆老爷》、《特务》、《在西方人的心目中》等，中篇小说《昧心》预测了20世纪许多大事的主题及后果。他的小说是改编电影和电视剧最受欢迎的题材。

Youth is life's seed-time.

O. W. Holmes, American physician and writer

青年时代是人生的播种期。

——霍尔姆斯,美国医生、作家

Young men are apt to think themselves wise enough, as drunken men are apt to think themselves sober enough.

Philip Dormer Chesterfield,
British diplomat and writer

正如喝醉的人总认为自己非常清醒一样,年轻人总认为自己非常聪明。

——切斯特菲尔德,英国外交家、作家

The disappointment of mankind succeeds to the delusion of youth: let us hope that the heritage of old age is not despair.

Benjamin Disraeli, British statesman

青年时期充满幻想,继之而来的是成年时期的失望:但愿老年时期所承传的不是绝望。

——狄斯累利,英国政治家

Every day is a little life; every waking and rising a little birth; every fresh morning a little youth.

Arthur Schopenhauer, German philosopher

每天都是一个小小的生命周期;每一次醒来、每一次起床都是一次小小的诞生;每一个清新的早晨都是短短的一段青春。

——叔本华,德国哲学家

It is the turn for the youth today to march ahead along our path. Hope you will be greater and happier than us.

Romain Rolland, French writer

今天轮到你们了,年轻人,踏在我们的身体上面向前吧。但愿你们比我们更伟大、更幸福。

——罗曼·罗兰,法国作家

Marriage
婚姻

Where there is marriage without love, there will be love without marriage.

Benjamin Franklin,
American statesman, writer, and scientist

有没有爱情的婚姻,就会有没有婚姻的爱情。

——富兰克林,美国政治家、作家、科学家

Love: a temporary insanity, curable by marriage.

Ambrose Bierce, American journalist and writer

爱:暂时的精神错乱,由婚姻来治愈。

——比尔斯,美国记者、作家

A woman's thought runs before her actions.

William Shakespeare, British dramatist

女人的思想总是比行动跑得更快。

——莎士比亚,英国剧作家

Marriage is a lottery in which men stake their liberty and women their happiness.

De Rieux

婚姻是六合彩,男人为它赌上了自由,女人为它押上了幸福。

——德里克斯

Some men seem remarkable to the world in whom neither their wives nor their valets saw anything extraordinary.

Montaigne, French thinker and essayist

一些人在众人看来光彩夺目，而在他们的妻子和仆人眼里却是普普通通。

——蒙田，法国思想家、散文家

The meeting of two personalities is like the contact of two chemical substances: if there is any reaction, both are transformed.

Carl Jung, Swiss psychiatrist

两种人格的相遇犹如两种化学物质的接触，一旦发生反应，双方都将改变。

——荣格，瑞士精神病学家

There is only one thing to do for a man who is married to a woman who enjoys spending money, and that is to enjoy earning it.

Edgar Watson Howe, American journalist

娶了喜欢花钱的老婆，男人只有一个选择，那就是喜欢挣钱。

——埃德加·沃森·豪，美国记者

Men marry because they are tired; women because they are curious. Both are disappointed.

Charles Lamb, British essayist

男人因为疲倦而娶，女人因为好奇而嫁，结果都是失望。

——兰姆，英国散文家

Women, as they grow older, rely more and more on cosmetics. Men, as they grow older, rely more and more on a sense of humor.

George Jean Nathan, American drama critic

女人随着年龄的增长越来越依靠化妆品,而男人随着年龄的增长越来越依靠幽默感。

——内森,美国戏剧评论家

Marriage may be compared to a cage: the birds outside despair to get in, and those within despair to get out.

Montaigne, French thinker and essayist

婚姻像一个鸟笼:外面的鸟儿想飞进去,里面的鸟儿想飞出来。

——蒙田,法国思想家、散文家

To marry means to half one's right and double one's duty.

Arthur Schopenhauer, German philosopher

结婚意味着平分你的权益,倍增你的责任。

——叔本华,德国哲学家

Family
家庭

The family is the nucleus of civilization.

W. Durant, American historian and essayist

家庭是文明的核心。

——威尔·杜兰特,美国历史学家、散文家

Home is the place where, when you have to go there, it has to take you in.

Robert Frost, American poet

无论何时何地,家永远是向游子敞开大门的地方。

——弗罗斯特,美国诗人

My father had always said that there are four things a child needs—plenty of love, nourishing food, regular sleep, and lots of soap and water—and after those, what he needs most is some intelligent neglect.

Ivy Baker Priest, American stateswoman

我父亲总是说,一个孩子需要四样东西——充分的爱、有营养的食物、有规律的睡眠、大量的肥皂和水——然后,他最需要的是明智的放任。

——普里斯特,美国女政治家

Washington Irving

华盛顿·欧文（1783—1859）是美国历史上第一位享有国际声誉的作家。他出身于富商家庭，曾任美国驻伦敦使馆秘书和美国驻西班牙公使。他的作品以幽默风趣的笔调和富于幻想的浪漫色彩，描写和叙述了古老的风俗习惯、神话传说以及善良淳朴的旧式人物。其作品构思巧妙，文笔流畅，幽默诙谐，情景交融，别具一格。他一生著作等身，但流传最广的是《见闻杂记》（*The Sketch Book*），此书使他享誉欧美乃至世界文坛。

Pearl Buck

赛珍珠（1892—1973），美国女作家。笔名John Sedges，赛珍珠是她自己起的中文名字。她出生于西弗吉尼亚州，自幼生活在中国，最早期的几部小说均含有中国生活的色彩。她的小说《大地》（*The Good Earth*）于1932年获普利策奖，并于1938年获诺贝尔文学奖。她是唯一同时获此两项奖的女作家。1935年，她返回美国，写有多部反映美国当代风情的小说，如《爱国者》和《龙种》。她将《水浒》译为英文并取名《四海之内皆兄弟》（*All Men Are Brothers*），于1933年出版。

It was the policy of the good old gentlemen to make his children feel that home was the happiest place in the world; and I value this delicious home-feeling as one of the choicest gifts a parent can bestow.

Washington Irving, American Father of literature

让孩子感到家庭是世界上最幸福的地方,这是以往有涵养的大人明智的做法。这种美妙的家庭情感,在我看来,和大人赠给孩子们的那些最精致的礼物一样珍贵。

——欧文,美国文学之父

Some are kissing mothers and some are scolding mothers, but it is love just the same, and most mothers kiss and scold together.

Pearl Buck, American female writer

有些母亲经常亲吻孩子,有些母亲经常责骂孩子,然而她们爱孩子如出一辙,大多数的母亲既亲吻孩子又责备孩子。

——赛珍珠,美国女作家

The house of every one is to him as his castle and fortress.

E. Coke, British jurist

家对于每个人都是城堡和要塞。

——科克,英国法理学家

The mother's heart is the child's schoolroom.

Henry Ward Beecher,
American clergyman and writer

母亲的心是孩子的课堂。

——亨利·沃德·比彻,美国牧师、作家

All happy families are like one another; each unhappy family is unhappy in its own way.

Leo Tolstoy, Russian writer

所有幸福的家庭都是十分相似的,而每个不幸的家庭却各有各的不幸。

——托尔斯泰,俄国作家

The family is one of nature's masterpieces.

G. Santayana, American philosopher and poet

家庭是大自然创造的杰作之一。

——乔治·桑塔亚纳,美国哲学家、诗人

The family is the test of freedom: because the family is the only thing that the free man makes for himself and by himself.

G. K. Chesterton, British writer and critic

家庭是自由的测试标准:因为家庭是自由人为自己造就的唯一的东西。

——切斯特顿,英国作家、评论家

There must always be a struggle between a father and son, while one aims at power and the other at independence.

Samuel Johnson, British writer

父子之间总存在斗争,一方是为了权力,而另一方则是为了独立。

——塞缪尔·约翰逊,英国作家

Experts say you should never hit your children in anger. When is a good time? When you are feeling festive?

Roseanne, American actress

专家说不该在盛怒的时候打孩子,那什么时候好呢?当你高兴的时候吗?

——罗西尼,美国女演员

Parents must get across the idea that "I love you always, but sometimes I do not love your behavior".

Amy Vanderbilt, American authority on etiquette

当父母的一定要让孩子明白"我永远爱你,但有时候不喜欢你的行为"。

——艾米·范德比尔特,美国礼仪专家

The joys of parents are secret, and so are their griefs and fears: they cannot utter the one, nor they will utter the other.

Francis Bacon, British essayist and philosopher

父母的欢乐含而不露,他们的悲哀和担心亦是如此:他们无法说出欢乐,也无法说出心中的担忧和悲哀。

——培根,英国散文作家、哲学家

Something you consider bad may bring out your child's talents; something you consider good may stifle them.

F. R. de Chateaubriand,

French statesman and writer

你认为不好的事情可能会激发孩子潜在的才能,你认为好的事情可能会窒息孩子的活力。

——夏多布里昂,法国政治家、作家

Allow children to be happy in their own way, for what better way will they ever find?

Samuel Johnson, British writer

允许孩子们以自己的方式享受快乐，因为孩子们的方式是他们能找到的最好的方式。

——塞缪尔·约翰逊，英国作家

The best way to keep children at home is to make the atmosphere pleasant and let the air out of the tires.

Dorothy Parker, American female writer

让孩子留在家里的最好办法是创造轻松愉快的家庭气氛。

——多萝西·帕克，美国女作家

The more you love your children, the more care you should take to neglect them occasionally. The web of affection can be drawn too tight.

David Sutton, British editor

你越爱你的孩子，你越要偶尔有意识地不管他们。爱的网收得太紧会适得其反。

——大卫·萨顿，英国编辑

We love our home, though our feet can leave it, yet our hearts cannot.

O. W. Holmes, American physician and writer

我们爱自己的家，我们的脚可以离它而去，可我们的心却不能。

——霍尔姆斯，美国医生、作家

我喜欢的名人名言

Some of my favorite quotes that are not contained in this book are:

A successful career

事业与成功

如果一个人朝他的梦想自信地前进，

为他所想象的生活努力，

他将在平淡的生活中遇到意想不到的成功。

If one advances confidently in the direction of his dreams,

and endeavors to live the life he has imagined,

he will meet with a success unexpected in common hours.

Work

工作

Moral of the Work. In war：resolution. In defeat：defiance. In victory：magnanimity. In peace：goodwill.

Winston Churchill，British Prime Minister

工作中的道德规范：在战争中，果敢坚定；在失败时，傲然不屈；在胜利时，宽宏大量；在和平时，友好亲切。

——丘吉尔，英国首相

One machine can do the work of fifty ordinary men. No machine can do the work of one extraordinary man.

Elbert Hubbard，American writer

一部机器能完成50个平凡人的工作，但没有一部机器能完成一个不平凡的人的工作。

——哈伯德，美国作家

No task is a long one but on which one dare not start. It becomes a nightmare.

Charles Baudelaire，French poet

只要敢开始，完成总有期。久久不敢开始的工作如同梦魇。

——波德莱尔，法国诗人

Elbert Hubbard

哈伯德（1856—1915），美国作家。他生于伊利诺伊州。哈伯德在塔夫茨大学取得文学硕士之后，又攻读了法学博士，最后进入了哈佛大学，在那里从事教学、编辑和演讲工作。1893 年，他创建了“罗伊克罗夫特”艺人社团，并编辑过月刊《庸人》。由于哈伯德罕见的经营天赋和写作才华，名誉和金钱接踵而来，不久就闻名于世。他于 1899 年在月刊上刊登的《致加西亚的一封信》，用以阐述他组织工人社团的思想，在全世界流传，2000 年被美国《哈奇森年鉴》和《出版商周刊》评选为有史以来世界最畅销图书第六名。哈伯德的《致加西亚的信》及姊妹篇《怎样把信送给加西亚》、《自动自发》、《鼓舞人心的剪贴本》、《一生的智慧》等书中推崇的敬业、忠诚、勤奋、自信、主动性等思想观念影响了一代又一代人、一个国家又一个国家。

Charles Baudelaire

波德莱尔（1821—1867），法国象征派诗人。他生于巴黎，早年被家人送往印度，但他途中登岸。1842 年，他在返回巴黎途中与欧亚混血儿迪百尔邂逅，后者遂成为他的情人和创作灵感的来源，他同时把许多时间花在德拉克鲁瓦、马奈和杜米埃的画室里。他的杰作是诗集《恶之花》，尽管该诗因有违公众道德观而被起诉，但此书深受评论界的赞誉，其影响一直延续到 20 世纪。其后期作品有《人为的天堂》、《小诗与散文》，占据他内心主要地位的死亡、堕落和恐怖是他作品的基本特色。

Every calling is great when greatly pursued.

O. W. Holmes, American physician and writer

人们全身心投入的事业往往都是伟大的事业。

—— 霍尔姆斯，美国医生、作家

They are able because they think they are able.

Virgil, Ancient Roman poet

能干的人之所以能干是因为他们认为自己能干。

——维吉尔，古罗马诗人

The test of a vocation is the love of the drudgery it involves.

Anonymous

是否热爱一种职业就看是否喜欢其中的劳苦。

——佚名

There is harmony between work and play, both combined skillfully, life art is then in it.

Romain Rolland, French writer

在工作和游乐之间，存在着一种和谐，两者巧妙地结合起来，生活的艺术就在其中了。

——罗曼·罗兰，法国作家

Business first; pleasure afterwards.

William Makepeace Thackeray, British novelist

先工作，后欢乐。

——萨克雷，英国小说家

People often ask me if I know the secret of success, and if I could tell others how to make their dreams come true. My answer is, you do it by working.

Walt Disney, American businessman

人们时常问我是否晓得成功的诀窍,能否告诉别人怎样使他们的梦想成为现实。我的回答是:工作。

——迪斯尼,美国实业家

Work banishes those three great evils: boredom, vice, and poverty.

Voltaire, French thinker

工作撵跑三个魔鬼:无聊、堕落和贫穷。

——伏尔泰,法国思想家

Only those who have the patience to do simple things perfectly ever acquire the skill to do difficult things easily.

Friedrich Chiller, German dramatist and poet

只有有耐心圆满完成简单工作的人,才能够轻而易举地完成困难的工作。

——席勒,德国剧作家、诗人

The best preparation for good work tomorrow is to do good work today.

Elbert Hubbard, American writer

为明天做好工作的最好的准备,就是把今天的工作做好。

——哈伯德,美国作家

Happiness, I have discovered, is nearly always a rebound from hard work.

David Grayson, American journalist

我发现,辛勤工作几乎总是与幸福相连。

——格雷森,美国记者

The commonest form, one of the most often neglected, and the safest opportunity for the average man to seize, is hard work.

Arthur Brisbane, American editor

对常人而言,最普通、最易被忽视、最安全的机遇,就是努力工作。

——布里斯班,美国编辑

Let us grateful to Adam. He cut us out of the blessing of idleness and won for us the curse of labor.

Mark Twain, American writer

让我们都来感激亚当吧,他无意中赐福创造了我们,又为我们赢得了该死的劳动。

——马克·吐温,美国作家

Competition
竞争

When written in Chinese, the word "crisis" is composed of two characters—one represents danger and the other represents opportunity.

John F. Kennedy, American President

汉语里,"危机"这个词由两个字组成——一个代表危险,另一个代表机遇。

——约翰·肯尼迪,美国总统

Competition is easier to accept if you realize it is not act of aggression or abrasion. I've worked with my best friends in direct competition. Whatever you want in life, other people are going to want too. Believe in yourself enough to accept the idea that you have an equal right to it.

Diane Sawyer, Ameican journalist

如果你意识到竞争并不是一种侵略或摩擦的行为,竞争就易于接受了。我就曾和我的好友直接竞争过。一生中无论你想得到什么,别人也想要,一定要相信自己,这样你才会肯定自己也有同样的权利去争取。

——索耶,美国记者

Force and fraud are in war the two cardinal virtues.

Thomas Hobbes, British philosopher

实力与计谋是战争中的两种基本力量。

——霍布斯,英国哲学家

All the fun is locking horns with impossibilities.

Claes Oldenburg, American sculptor

有意思的是大家为不可能的事争斗得难解难分。

——奥登伯格,美国雕塑家

Compete, don't envy.

Arab proverb

要竞争,不要嫉妒。

——阿拉伯谚语

A nation that lacks the spirit for progress means degeneration. Only through pioneering and competition can it stand undefeated.

A. N. Whitehead,
British mathematician and philosopher

缺乏进取精神的民族意味着堕落。唯有开拓和竞争,才能立于不败之地。

——怀特海,英国数学家、哲学家

Claes Oldenburg

奥登伯格（1929— ），美国雕塑家。他生于斯德哥尔摩，先后在耶鲁大学和芝加哥美术学院求学，1956 年迁居纽约，投身于正在兴起的流行艺术运动。1963 年，他推出采用灯光及开关之类日常硬物品镶入软雕塑的新艺术，以此闻名遐迩。人们在公众场所有时会看到他所制作的大型的不朽作品。

Alfred North Whitehead

怀特海（1861—1947），英国数学家、唯心主义哲学家。他生于肯特郡拉姆斯盖特，就读于剑桥大学，毕业后任多家知名学府教授。1910 年，他与弟子罗素合著《数学原理》，其他作品有《观念的历险》和《思维方式》等。

Cooperation
合作

Everyone needs help from everyone.

Bertolt Brecht, German poet and dramatist

人人都需要他人的帮助。

——布莱希特，德国诗人、剧作家

Certainly absolute freedom would be more beautiful if we were birds or poets; but cooperation and a loving sacrifice of part of ourselves are beautiful too, if we are men living together.

George Santayana,
American philosopher and poet

当然，完全的自由更为美丽，倘若我们是小鸟或是诗人；但是合作，满含深情地作出一部分牺牲也同样美丽，倘若我们是邻居。

——乔治·桑塔亚那，美国哲学家、诗人

People need to know one another to be at their honest best.

Robbins Staca, British writer

人们需要相互了解才能达到最诚实的境界。

——斯达卡，英国作家

Mutual forgiveness of each vice, such are the gates of Paradise.

William Black, British poet

彼此宽容对方的缺点,乃是通向天堂之门。

——布莱克,英国诗人

Nobody can avoid coming into conflicts with others. He has to push through the crowd in different ways, offending others while being offended.

Thomas Carlyle, British writer

没有人在生活中能不与别人碰撞。他不得不以各种方式奋力挤过人群,冒犯别人的同时也忍受别人的冒犯。

——卡莱尔,英国作家

No man is useless in this world who lightens the burden of someone else.

Charles Dickens, British writer

世上能为别人减轻负担的人都是有用的。

——狄更斯,英国作家

The law of life should not be the competition of acquisitiveness, but cooperation, the good of each contributing to the good of all.

Assed

生活的法则应当不是竞相索取,而是合作,是人人把自己的幸福奉献给众人。

——阿萨德

Everything that lives, lives not alone, nor for itself.

William Black, British poet

世上的一切事物,既非孤立存在,亦非只为自身生存。

——布莱克,英国诗人

In almost every face and every person, they may discover fine feathers and defects, good and bad qualities.

Benjamin Franklin,
American statesman, writer, and scientist

人各有其面,有优缺点,有长短处。

——富兰克林,美国政治家、作家、科学家

No matter how great one's power is, if he cooperates with others, he will give fuller scope than does it alone.

Samuel Butler, British writer

不管一个人的力量大小,他要跟大家合作,总比一个人能发挥更大的作用。

——塞缪尔·巴特勒,英国作家

Never hate your enemy. It affects your judgment.

Mario Puzo, American writer

千万不要恨你的敌人,那会影响你的判断力。

——马里奥·普佐,美国作家

We can learn even from our enemies.

Ovid, Ancient Roman poet

我们甚至可以向敌人学习。

——奥维德,古罗马诗人

If you would go up high, then use your own legs! Do not let yourselves carried aloft; do not seat yourselves on other people's backs and heads.

F. W. Nietzsche, German Philosopher

如果你想走到高处,就要使用自己的两条腿!不要让别人把你抬到高处;不要坐在别人的背上和头上。

——尼采,德国哲学家

Every kind of peaceful cooperation among men is primarily based on mutual trust and only secondly on institutions such as courts of justice and police.

Albert Einstein, American scientist

人类一切和平合作的基础首先是相互信任,其次才是法庭和警察一类的机构。

——爱因斯坦,美国科学家

Cooperation is power; in proportion as people combine, they know their strength.

Lytton, British writer and statesman

合作就是力量;人民联合得越紧密,他们就越认识到自己的强大。

——利顿,英国作家、政治家

If you would convince others, you seem open to conviction yourself.

Philip Dormer Chesterfield, British statesman

要说服别人,先得说服自己。

——切斯特菲尔德,英国政治家

To ask for advice is, in nine cases out of ten, to tout for flattery.

Anonymous

绝大多数情况下,寻求建议就是寻求恭维。

——佚名

There are things which it is not only impossible to discuss intelligently, but which it is not even intelligent to discuss.

Dostoyevsky, Russian writer

有些事情不仅不可能进行明智的讨论,而且拿出来讨论都是不明智的。

——陀思妥耶夫斯基,俄国作家

Words divide us; action unites us.

Tupamaros

语言使我们分裂,行动使我们团结。

——图帕马罗斯

You cannot shake hands with a clenched fist.

Indira Gandhi, Indian stateswoman

你无法与紧握的拳头握手。

——英迪拉·甘地,印度女政治家

Dostoyevsky

陀思妥耶夫斯基（1821—1881），俄国小说家，出身于莫斯科一个医生家庭，早年为军事工程师，后投身文学创作。因在彼得堡参加革命，1849 年他被送到西伯利亚做苦役，1859 年回到圣彼得堡。流放回来后，他的创作重点逐渐转向心理悲剧，写出了杰作《罪与罚》，这是最有力的现实主义文学作品之一，使他获得了世界声誉。其他重要作品有《白痴》、《被伤害与被侮辱的人们》、《卡拉马佐夫兄弟》等。最后一部作品《卡拉马佐夫兄弟》是作者哲学思考的总结。陀思妥耶夫斯基的善恶矛盾性格组合，深层心理活动描写都对后世作家产生了深刻的影响。

Success
成功

There is only one success—to be able to spend your life in your own way.

Christopher Morley, American writer

人生只有一种成功,那就是能够用自己的方式度过自己的一生。

——克里斯托弗·莫利,美国作家

The human being longs for a sense of being accomplished, of being able to do things, with his hand, with his mind, with his will. Each of us wants to feel he or she has the ability to do something that is meaningful and that serves a tribute to our inherent abilities.

Leonard R. Saylis, British writer

人们渴求有一种成就感,渴望有能力用自己的手、用自己的脑、用自己的意志办事。我们每个人都希望自己能够作出有意义、并能显示出自己天赋的事来。

——塞尔斯,英国作家

Failure is not our only punishment for laziness; there is also the success of others.

Jules Renard, French writer

对于懒惰的惩罚不仅仅是自己的失败,还有别人的成功。

——朱尔斯·雷纳,法国作家

The line between failure and success is so fine that we scarcely know when we pass it：so fine that we are often on the line and do not know it.

Elbert Hubbard，American writer

失败与成功的界线如此微妙，我们跨过它时极少察觉，以至我们往往意识不到自己就处在这条线上。

——哈伯德，美国作家

Affairs succeed by patience；and he that is hasty fallen headlong.

Sadi，Iranian poet

事业成于坚韧，毁于急躁。

——萨迪，伊朗诗人

When we can begin to take our failures non-seriously，it means we are ceasing to be afraid of them. It is of immense importance to learn to laugh at ourselves.

Katherine Mansfield，British female writer

当我们不把失败当回事，这就意味着我们不再畏惧它。学会自嘲是至关重要的一步。

——凯瑟林·曼斯菲尔德，英国女作家

Small opportunities are often the beginning of great enterprises.

Demosthenes，Ancient Greek orator

微小的机会常常是伟大事业的开始。

——狄摩西尼，古希腊演讲家

It never will rain roses. When we want to have more roses we must plant trees.

G. Eliot, British female writer

天上永远不会掉下玫瑰,如果想要更多的玫瑰,必须自己种植。

——乔治·艾略特,英国女作家

No pain, no palm; no thorns, no throne; no gall, no glory; no cross, no crown.

William Penn, British settler

没有辛劳就没有胜利;没有荆棘就没有王位;没有勇气就没有光荣;没有苦难(十字架)就没有王冠。

——威廉·佩恩,英国殖民者

The prime condition of success, the great secret is concentrated your energy, thought and capital exclusively upon the business in which you are engaged.

Andrew Carnegie,
American industrialist and the King of Steel

成功的基本条件和关键的秘诀是:集中精力、思想和资金,一心一意地做事。

——安德鲁·卡耐基,美国实业家、钢铁大王

To accomplish great things, we must not only act, but also dream; not only plan, but also believe.

Anatole France, French novelist and critic

为了成就一番事业,我们不仅要行动,还要梦想;不仅要规划,还要坚信。

——法朗士,法国小说家、文艺批评家

William Penn

威廉·佩恩（1644—1718），贵格会改革派教徒和殖民者，宾夕法尼亚的创建人。他生于伦敦，因反对圣公会礼仪被牛津大学开除。1666 年，他参加贵格会，1668 年因写文章被捕入狱，在伦敦塔里写成了他最著名的一本书《没有十字，没有王冠》（*No Cross*, *No Crown*）。1681 年，他在北美洲得到一块土地，为纪念他的父亲海军上将佩恩爵士，将这块土地定名为宾夕法尼亚，他统治这块殖民地达两年。

Andrew Carnegie

安德鲁·卡耐基（1835—1919），20 世纪初美国最成功的商人之一，美国商业精神的创立者。他出生于苏格兰邓弗姆林，1848 年随全家移民美国宾夕法尼亚州。13 岁起，他外出做工，做过纺织厂的绕线工、信差、电报员。在美国“镀金时代”的大背景下，他依靠个人奋斗兴办铁路、开采石油，并最终投身钢铁业，成为美国工业发展史上的“钢铁大王”，与洛克菲勒、摩根并立成为当时美国经济界的三大巨头。卡耐基为现代人树立了财富准则，他晚年致力于慈善事业，热衷图书馆及各项公共事业的捐赠，并在生前将自己的全部财产捐献一空。

You have to believe in yourself. That's the secret of success.

Charles Chaplin, American actor

自信,是成功的秘诀。

——卓别林,美国演员

Achievement provides the only real pleasure in life.

Thomas Edison, American inventor

有所成就是人生唯一的真正乐趣。

——爱迪生,美国发明家

Will, work and wait are the pyramidal cornerstones for success.

Louis Pasteur, French chemist

意志、工作和等待是成功的金字塔的基石。

——巴斯德,法国化学家

Victory won't come to me unless I go to it .

M. Moore, American female poet

胜利不会向我走来,我必须自己走向胜利。

——穆尔,美国女诗人

I succeeded because I willed it; I never hesitated.

Bonapart Napoleon, French Emperor

我成功是因为我有决心,从不踌躇。

——拿破仑,法国皇帝

Success covers a multitude of blunders.

George Bernard Shaw, British dramatist

成功由大量的失误铸就。

——萧伯纳,英国剧作家

Few things are impossible in themselves; and it is often for want of will, rather than of means, that man fails to succeed.

La Rochefoucauld, French writer

事情很少有根本做不成的;其所以做不成,与其说是条件不够,不如说是由于决心不够。

——拉罗什福科,法国作家

Before everything else, getting ready is the secret of success.

Henry Ford, American manufacturer

做好准备是成功的首要秘诀。

——亨利·福特,美国制造商

I have learned, that if one advances confidently in the direction of his dreams, and endeavors to live the life he has imagined, he will meet with a success unexpected in common hours.

H. D. Thoreau, American writer and philosopher

我已经了解,如果一个人朝他的梦想自信地前进,为他所想象的生活努力,他将在平淡的生活中遇到意想不到的成功。

——梭罗,美国作家、思想家

William (Bill) H. Gates

比尔·盖茨（1955— ），美国微软公司董事长。他出生于西雅图，13岁就开始编写计算机程序。1973年，盖茨进入哈佛大学，为第一台微型计算机——MITSAltair开发了BASIC编程语言。大学三年级时，盖茨从哈佛退学，与童年伙伴Paul Allen一起创建了微软公司。他们深信个人计算机将是每一部办公桌面系统以及每一个家庭非常有价值的工具，并为这一信念所指引，开始为个人计算机开发软件。在盖茨的领导下，微软的使命是不断地提高和改进软件技术，并使人们更加轻松、更经济有效而且更有趣味地使用计算机。1995年，他出版了《未来之路》（*The Road Ahead*），曾经连续七周名列纽约时报畅销书排行榜的榜首。从退学建立微软，到成为世界首富，盖茨只用了20年的时间，被美国人誉为“坐在世界巅峰的人”。盖茨把他的大量个人财富捐献给了慈善事业。据统计，盖茨至今已为世界各地的慈善事业捐出近290亿美元的财富，成为世界上最慷慨的富人。盖茨是一个书迷，而且很喜欢打高尔夫和桥牌。

Thomas Edison

爱迪生（1847—1931），美国电学家和发明家。他生于美国俄亥俄州一个农民家庭，由母亲辅导他自学，16岁时发明了自动定时发报机，之后不断有发明问世。1928年，他被授予美国国会金质特别奖章。他除了在留声机、电灯、电话、电报、电影等方面的发明和贡献以外，在矿业、建筑业、化工等领域也有不少著名的创造和真知灼见。爱迪生一生共有约两千项创造发明，为人类的文明和进步作出了巨大贡献。1931年爱迪生逝世，全美国熄灯以示哀悼。

Always bear in mind that your own resolution to succeed is more important than any other thing.

Abraham Lincoln, American President

永远记住:你自己取得成功的决心比什么都重要。

——林肯,美国总统

A man can succeed at almost anything for which he has unlimited enthusiasm.

C. M. Schwab, American businessman

无论何事,只要对它有无限的热情你就能成功。

——施瓦布,美国实业家

If you wish to succeed, you should use persistence as your good friend, experience as your reference, prudence as your brother and hope as your sentry.

Thomas Edison, American inventor

如果你希望成功,当以恒心为良友,以经验为参谋,以谨慎为兄弟,以希望为哨兵。

——爱迪生,美国发明家

The world won't care about your self-esteem. The world will expect you to accomplish something before you feel good about yourself.

William (Bill) H. Gates, Chairman of Microsoft

这世界并不会在意你的自尊。这世界指望你在自我感觉良好之前先要有所成就。

——比尔·盖茨,美国微软公司董事长

What is the man's first duty? The answer is brief: to be himself.

Henrik Ibsen, Norwegian dramatist

一个人首要的职责是什么？答案很简单:做他自己。

——易卜生,挪威剧作家

Do not, for one repulse, give up the purpose that you resolved to effect.

William Shakespeare, British dramatist and poet

不要只因一次失败,就放弃你原来决心想达到的目的。

——莎士比亚,英国剧作家、诗人

There are but two roads that lead to an important goal and to the doing of great things: strength and perseverance. Strength is the lot of but a few privileged men; but austere perseverance, harsh and continuous, may be employed by the smallest of us and rarely fails of its purpose, for its silent power grows irresistibly greater with time.

John Walfgang Von Goethe, German writer

世间只有两条路,可以使人达到重大目标或完成伟业,那就是力量和坚持不懈。力量只有少数得天独厚的人才能拥有,但严格而坚持不懈,是任何最渺小的人物都能做得到的,且很少有不能达到目的的时候,因为坚持不懈的静默力量随着时间而变得强大起来,不可抗拒。

——歌德,德国作家

A man can fail many times, but he isn't a failure until he begins to blame somebody else.

W. S. Burroughs, American writer

一个人可以失败许多次,但只要他没开始责怪别人,他就不是一个失败者。

——伯勒斯,美国作家

A failure is a man who has blundered but who is not able to cash in the experience.

Elbert Hubbard, American writer

一个失败的人是一个犯了错误又不能从中吸取教训的人。

——哈伯德,美国作家

The greatest of faults is to be conscious of none.

Thomas Carlyle, British writer

最严重的错误莫过于不觉得自己有任何错误。

——卡莱尔,英国作家

The failure and reverses which await men—and one after another sadden the brow of youth—add the dignity to the prospect of human life, which no Arcadian success would do.

Henry David Thoreau,
American writer and thinker

尽管失败和挫折等待着人们,一次次地夺走青春的容颜,但却给人生的前途增添一份尊严,这是任何顺利的成功都不能做到的。

——梭罗,美国作家、思想家

There is the greatest practical benefit in making a few failures early in life.

T. Huxley, British biologist

在人生起步的时候遭到几次失败有绝大的实际益处。

——赫胥黎,英国生物学家

The key to successful leadership today is influence, not authority.

Kenneth Blanchard,
American business consultant

今天成功领导的关键是影响力,而非权力。

——布兰查德,美国商业顾问

Only those who have the patience to do simple things perfectly ever acquire the skill to do difficult things easily.

Friedrich Schiller, German dramatist and poet

只有有耐心圆满完成简单工作的人,才能够轻而易举地完成困难的事。

——席勒,德国剧作家、诗人

The people who get on in this world are the people who get up and look for circumstances they want, and if they cannot find them, they make them.

George Bernard Shaw, British dramatist

在这个世界上,取得成功的人是那些努力寻找他们想要机会的人,如果找不到机会,他们就去创造机会。

——萧伯纳,英国剧作家

If you would hit the mark, you must aim a little above it. Every arrow that flies feels the attraction of earth.

Longfellow, America poet

要想射中靶,必须瞄得比靶略为高些,因为脱弦之箭都受到地心引力的影响。

——朗费罗,美国诗人

Perseverance is a great element of success; if you only knock long enough and loud enough at the gate, you are sure to wake up somebody.

Longfellow, American poet

持之以恒是成功的要素:在通往成功的门口,只要你坚持使劲地敲门,就一定会有人被唤醒。

——朗费罗,美国诗人

Wealth
财富

Property is an intellectual production. The game requires coolness, right reasoning, promptness, and patience in the players.

Ralph Waldo Emerson, American thinker

财产是智力的产物，其追逐者需要有清醒的头脑、准确的推理、敏捷的反应和必要的耐心。

——爱默生，美国思想家

Few rich men own their property. The property owns them.

Robert Green Ingersoll, American lawyer

极少有富人拥有他们的财产，是财产拥有他们。

——英格索尔，美国律师

Money may be the husk of many things, but not the kernel. It brings you food, but not appetite; medicine, but not health; acquaintances, but not friends; servants, but not loyalty; days of joy, but not peace of happiness.

Ibsen, Norwegian dramatist

金钱可以是许多东西的外壳，却不是核心。它带来食物，却带不来胃口；带来药，却带不来健康；带来相识，却带不来友谊；带来仆人，却带不来忠心；带来享受，却带不来幸福的宁静。

——易卜生，挪威剧作家

I finally know what distinguishes man from the other beasts: financial worries.

Jules Renard, French playwright

我终于明白了人与野兽的区别:人为钱而担忧。

——勒纳尔,法国剧作家

A bargain is something you can't use but which is so cheap you can't afford not to buy it.

Herbert Prochnow,

American banking executive, master of ceremonies, and writer

便宜的东西是你用不着,但又便宜得让你不得不买的东西。

——赫伯特·普罗克诺,

美国金融家、主持人、作家

It is better to live rich than to die rich.

Samuel Johnson, British writer

与其死时家财万贯,不如活得丰富多彩。

——约翰逊,英国作家

It is good to have money to buy things that money can buy, but it is better not to lose things money cannot buy.

George H. Lorimer, American journalist

有钱去买钱能买到的东西当然不错,但不丢失金钱买不到的东西更好。

——洛里默,美国记者

There are two times in a man's life when he should not speculate—when he can't afford it, and when he can.

Mark Twain, American writer

人的一生中有两个时刻不应当投机:一个是当他没钱时,另一个是当他有钱时。

——马克·吐温,美国作家

I've never been poor, only broke. Being poor is a frame of mind. Being broke is only a temporary situation.

Mike Todd, American producer

我从未贫穷过,只是破产过。受穷是一种心境,而破产只是暂时的情形。

——麦克·托德,美国制片人

Put in its proper place, money is not man's enemy, not his undoing, nor his master. It is his servant, and it must be made to serve him well.

Henry Alexander Murray, American psychologist

用在合适的地方,金钱不是人类的敌人,不是人类的毁灭者,也不是人类的主人,而是人类的奴仆,它必须服侍好人类。

——亨利·墨瑞,美国心理学家

There is pain in getting, care in keeping, and grief in losing riches.

Thomas Draxe, British clergyman

得财艰辛,守财费心,失财痛心。

——德雷克斯,英国牧师

Mike Todd

麦克·托德（1909—1958），美国制片人。他生于明尼苏达州，1927 年前往好莱坞，1933 年在芝加哥世界博览会期间表演了一种真正的“时事讽刺舞剧”，后开始制作戏剧、音乐喜剧和电影。他最先采用称作“托德—AO”的三维宽银幕电影技术，并以此制作了影片《八十天环游地球》，该片 1956 年获奥斯卡奖。1957 年，他与电影女演员泰勒结婚，成为她的第三任丈夫，但翌年在一场空难中丧生。

Wealth unused might as well not exist.

Aesop, Ancient Greek fable writer

有财富不用等于没有财富。

——伊索，古希腊寓言作家

Sometimes one pays most for the things one gets for nothing.

Albert Einstein, American scientist

人有时为无偿得到的东西付出的代价最高。

——爱因斯坦，美国科学家

Money is not the root of all evils as is usually claimed, what is the root of all evils is the lust for money, that is the excessive, selfish and greedy pursuit of money.

Nathaniel Hawthorne, American writer

金钱并非像人们常说的那样是万恶之源，对金钱的贪欲，即对金钱过分的、自私的、贪婪的追求，才是一切邪恶的根源。

——霍桑，美国作家

A penny saved is a penny gained.

Richard Brokminster Fuller, American architect

省下一分钱等于挣到一分钱。

——富勒，美国建筑师

Frugality is a handsome income.

Erasmus, Dutch humanist

节俭是一笔可观的收入。

——伊拉斯谟，荷兰人文主义者

The only thing wealth does for some people is to make them worry about losing them.

Rivarol, French writer

财富对有些人来说只是让他们担心失去。

——里瓦罗尔，法国作家

One of the difficult takes in this world is to convince a woman that even a bargain costs money.

Edgar Watson Howe, American journalist

世界上最难的事情之一是让女人相信便宜的东西也是要花钱的。

——埃德加·沃森·豪，美国记者

If we command our wealth, we shall be rich and free, if our wealth commands us, we are poor indeed.

Edmund Burke, British statesman

如果我们能支配财富，我们就会变得富裕、自由；如果财富支配了我们，我们则一贫如洗。

——伯克，英国政治家

Be not penny-wise: riches have wings, and sometimes they fly away of themselves; sometimes they must be set flying to bring in more.

Francis Bacon, British essayist and philosopher

不要斤斤计较：财富长有翅膀，有时会自己飞走，有时必须让它飞走以挣得更多的财富。

——培根，英国散文作家、哲学家

Never buy what you do not want because it is cheap; it will be dear to you.

Thomas Jefferson, American President

不要因为便宜而买你并不需要的东西,它将对你非常昂贵。

——杰弗逊,美国总统

One is not rich by what one owns, but more by what one is able to do without with dignity.

Immanuel Kant, German philosopher

一个人的富有并不凭着他所拥有的东西,而更凭着那些他可以没有但仍保持着尊严的东西。

——康德,德国哲学家

What costs little is little worth.

Baltasar Gracián, Spanish philosopher and writer

便宜没好货。

——格雷西安,西班牙哲学家、作家

Seek not proud riches, but such as thou mayest get justly, use soberly, distribute cheerfully, and leave contentedly.

Francis Bacon,
British essayist and philosopher

不要寻求令人称羡的财富,应当追求这样的境界:对财富正当地获取,清醒地使用,愉快地施舍,并能知足地放弃。

——培根,英国散文作家、哲学家

我喜欢的名人名言

Some of my favorite quotes that are not contained in this book are:

Connected with the World

我们都应当关心未来，

因为我们今后的生活将在那里度过。

We should all be concerned about the future because

we will have to spend the rest of our lives there

Society
社会

A general definition of civilization: a civilized society is exhibiting the five qualities of Truth, Beauty, Adventure, Art, and Peace.

A. N. Whitehead,
British mathematician and philosopher

文明的大意是,一个文明社会应表现出真实、美好、进取、艺术与和平这五个特性。

——怀特海,英国数学家、哲学家

Social prosperity means man happy, the citizen free, the nation great.

Victor Hugo, French writer

社会繁荣意味着人民幸福、公民自由、国家伟大。

——雨果,法国作家

I suppose society is wonderfully delightful. To be in it is merely a bore. But to be out of it is simply a tragedy.

Oscar Wilde, British writer

我认为社会非常有趣。置身其中,实在令人讨厌,但是如果置身其外,则简直是一场悲剧。

——王尔德,英国作家

There are no warlike peoples; just warlike leaders.

Ralph Bunche, American diplomat

没有好战的人民,只有好战的领袖。

——拉尔夫·邦奇,美国外交家

A diplomat is one who can cut his neighbor's throat without his neighbor noticing it.

Carlos P. Romulo, Philippine statesman,

外交官是能在对方不知不觉的情况下置对方于死地的人。

——卡洛斯 P. 罗慕洛,菲律宾政治家

The world can be changed by man's endeavor, and that this endeavor can lead to something new and better. No man can sever the bonds that unite him to his society simply by averting his eyes. He must ever be receptive and sensitive to the new; and have sufficient courage and skill to novel facts and to deal with them.

Franklin Roosevelt, American President

人经过努力可以改变世界,这种努力可以使人类达到新的、更美好的境界。没有人仅凭闭目、不看社会现实就能割断自己与社会的联系。他必须敏感,随时准备接受新鲜事物;他必须有勇气与能力去面对新的事实,解决新问题。

——罗斯福,美国总统

The world either breaks or hardens the heart.

Nicolas Chamfort, French writer

这个世界要么使你变得铁石心肠,要么使你心碎。

——尚福,法国作家

Henry Kissinger

基辛格（1923— ），美国国务卿和学者。他生于德国，他的一家因不堪纳粹对犹太人的迫害，于1938年移居美国。他就读于哈佛大学，战争期间在美军服役，后在政府一些机构任职，1962～1972年在哈佛大学执教。1969年，他任尼克松政府的国家安全事务助理，是结束越战谈判中美方的主要人物（因此与他人共获1973年诺贝尔和平奖），先后在尼克松政府和福特政府中任国务卿。他通过“穿梭外交”促进了以色列与阿拉伯国家间的和谈，使以色列和埃及的关系得到明显改善。他于1977年离任后，创建了咨询机构基辛格协会。

Ernest Hemingway

欧内斯特·海明威（1899—1961），美国小说家。他出身于伊利诺伊州一医生家庭，中学毕业后来到堪萨斯市担任《明星报》记者。1937年，投身西班牙反法西斯斗争。20世纪40年代初，他曾来到中国报道抗日战争。1954年，获诺贝尔文学奖，1961年，用猎枪自杀。他的长篇小说《太阳照常升起》，描写战后一批流落欧洲的青年内心的迷惘、彷徨和幻灭感，被看作是“迷惘的一代”的代表作。其他主要作品有长篇小说《永别了，武器》、《丧钟为谁而鸣》，中篇小说《老人与海》等。

The reason for having diplomatic relations is not to confer a compliment, but to secure a convenience.

Winston Churchill, British Prime Minister

建立外交关系并不是为了表达敬意,而是为了取得方便。

——丘吉尔,英国首相

The absence of alternatives clears the mind marvelously.

Henry Kissinger, American statesman

缺少选择余地可以极大地理清思想。

——基辛格,美国政治家

The first panacea for a mismanaged nation is inflation of the currency. The second is war. Both bring a temporary prosperity; both bring a permanent ruin.

Ernest Hemingway, American writer

对于一个治理不善的国家来说,最好的灵丹妙药就是通货膨胀,其次是战争。它们都能带来暂时的繁荣,也都能带来永久的毁灭。

——海明威,美国作家

My fellow Americans, ask not what your country can do for you; ask what you can do for your country. My fellow citizens of the world; ask not what America will do for you, but what together we can do for the freedom of man.

John Kennedy, American President

美国同胞们,不要问国家能为你们做些什么,而要问你们能为国家做些什么。全世界的公民们,不要问美国将为你们做些什么,而要问我们共同能为人类的自由做些什么。

——约翰·肯尼迪,美国总统

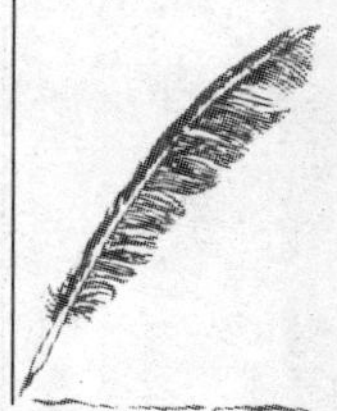

All history is the propaganda of the victorious.

Anonymous

所有的历史都是胜利者的宣传。

——佚名

Lying disguises our mortality, our inadequacies, our fears and anxieties, our loneliness in the midst of the crowd. We yearn for the comfort of familiar lies to create a more amenable reality.

Howards Mel, *American writer*

说谎掩盖了人死的必然性、缺陷、恐惧、焦虑和在熙熙攘攘的人群中所感到的孤独。耳熟能详的谎言会创造一个较易应付的现实。人渴望从这些谎言中得到安慰。

——梅尔,美国作家

We refute praise from a desire to be praised twice.

La Rochefoucauld, *French writer*

我们“谦虚地”驳斥别人对我们的赞扬,是希望对方重复他们的赞扬。

——拉罗什富科,法国作家

Force, violence, pressure, or compulsion with a view to conformity are both uncivilized and undemocratic.

Mahatma Gandhi, *Indian statesman*

以权势、暴力、压力或强迫的方式让人们意见一致,既不文明也不民主。

——圣雄甘地,印度政治家

Let me smile with the wise and eat with the rich.

Samuel Johnson, British writer

让我同智者一起微笑，同富人一起吃饭。

——塞缪尔·约翰逊，英国作家

A conservative is a man who just sits and thinks mostly sits.

Woodrow Wilson, American President

保守者是大部分时间坐着，个别时候空想的人。

——威尔逊，美国总统

A celebrity is a person who works hard all his life to become well-known, then wears dark glasses to avoid being recognized.

Fred Allen Wolf, American physicist

名人是一辈子拼命工作想出名，出名后又戴上墨镜以防被认出来的人。

——弗雷德·艾伦·沃尔夫，美国物理学家

The art of progress is to preserve order amid change and to preserve change amid order.

A. N. Whitehead,
British mathematician and philosopher

进步的艺术是在变革中保持秩序，在秩序中进行变革。

——怀特海，英国数学家、哲学家

John Arbuthnot

约翰·阿巴思诺特（1667—1735），英国医生和作家，生于格兰扁的因弗伯维。因为他本身是名医、医学著作的作者和安妮女王的御医，使其成为斯威夫特和当时所有文学名流的亲密朋友。1712 年，他出版了 5 本讽刺马尔伯勒公爵的小册子，后合成一本书名为《约翰牛传》（*The History of John Bull*），这是“约翰牛”成为典型英国人形象的起源。

Charles Kettering

凯特林（1876—1958），美国发明家。他生于俄亥俄州，1904 年研制出第一台电动现金出纳机，继而与人共创戴顿工程实验室，早年发明的电启动器为汽车工业带来一场革命。他的成就包括对飞机设计、燃料和柴油机的改进。他一生投身科学，从建立斯隆－凯特林癌症研究所到创建凯特林基金会，达到事业的顶峰。

Arnold Toynbee

阿诺德·汤因比（1852—1883），英国经济学家和社会改革家。他生于伦敦，在牛津大学执教经济史，并为多届成年工人教育班授课，与巴尼特一道在伦敦东区从事社会工作。使他最负盛名的是写出《英国的产业革命》（*The Industrial Revolution in England*，1884）一书和创造了“产业革命”一词。伦敦的“汤因比服务所”就是为纪念他而于1885 年创办的。

All political parties die at last of swallowing their own lies.

John Arbuthnot, British physician and writer

所有的政党最终都毁于言而无信。

——阿巴思诺特，英国医生、作家

The danger of the past was that men became slaves. The danger of the future is that men may become robots.

Erich Fromm,
German psychiatrist and philosopher

过去人们怕成为奴隶，将来人们可能怕成为机器人。

——埃里克·弗罗姆，
德国精神病学家和哲学家

Civilization is a movement and not a condition, a voyage and not a harbor.

Arnold Toynbee,
British economist and social reformer

文明是发展不是状况，是航行不是港口。

——阿诺德·汤因比，
英国经济学家、社会改革家

We should all be concerned about the future because we will have to spend the rest of our lives there.

Charles Kettering, American inventor

我们都应当关心未来，因为我们今后的生活将在那里度过。

——查尔斯·凯特林，美国发明家

A new vision of development is emerging. Development is becoming a people-centered process, whose ultimate goal must be the improvement of the human condition.

Boutros Boutros Ghali, Egyptian statesman, and
The sixth Secretary General of the United Nations

一个新的发展前景正在展现，发展正在变成一个以人民为中心的过程，其最终目的是改善人类的生存状况。

——布特罗斯·布特罗斯·加利，
埃及政治家、联合国第六任秘书长

Boutros Boutros – Ghali

加利（1922— ），联合国第六任秘书长（1992—1996）。加利出身于埃及开罗的一个基督教家庭，他的家族中有一位前埃及首相布特罗斯·加利（埃及首相）（1846—1910）。加利于1946年毕业于开罗大学，并获得了巴黎大学国际法博士的学位，国际关系学的毕业证书。此后直到1977年，他是开罗大学的国际法以及国际关系的教授。他于1973年步入政界，1974年至1977年，他担任阿拉伯社会主义联盟中央委员会和政治局成员。。在1977年至1991年期间，他担任埃及外交国务部长。1991年12月联合国大会任命加利为联合国第六任秘书长，任期五年，他成为联合国历史上第一位担任此职务的非洲人。加利的继任者是科菲·安南，这是由于加利没能连任，所以他的继任者需从其代表的非洲选出。加利出版有两本回忆录——《通往耶路撒冷的埃及之路》、《不屈不挠：美国—联合国的传奇》。

Nature
自然

Nature never deceives us; it is we who deceive ourselves.

***Rousseau**, French thinker*

自然界从不欺骗我们,欺骗我们的是我们自己。

——卢梭,法国思想家

When one tugs at a single thing in nature, he finds it attached to the rest of the world.

***John Muir**, American explorer and naturalist*

不管你触动自然界的任何事物,总会发现它与世界上的其他东西有着千丝万缕的关系。

——缪尔,美国探险家、博物学家

Animals are such agreeable friends—they ask no questions, they pass no criticisms.

***George Eliot**, British female writer*

动物是极容易相处的,它们从不提问,也从不会批评。

——乔治·艾略特,英国女作家

To waste, to destroy, our natural resources, to skin and exhaust the land instead of using it so as to increase its usefulness, will result in undermining in the days of our children the very prosperity which we ought by right to hand down to them amplified and developed.

Theodore Roosevelt, *American President*

对于本应开发扩展造福后代的土地和自然资源,我们不仅没有有效利用以增加其价值,反而浪费破坏,损毁殆尽,这必将摧毁子孙后代的繁荣。

——西奥多·罗斯福,美国总统

Everything beautiful has its moments and then passes away.

Luis Cernuda, *Spanish poet*

美丽的事物都会在经历其最美的时刻后消亡。

——路易·塞纽达,西班牙诗人

Peace
和平

Peace is liberty in tranquility.

Cicero, Ancient Roman statesman and orator

和平是宁静的自由。

——西塞罗，古罗马政治家、演说家

The goal of war is peace; of business, leisure.

Aristotle, Ancient Greek philosopher

战争的目的是和平；劳动的目的是休闲。

——亚里士多德，古希腊哲学家

We must go on to do all in our power to conquer the doubts and the fears, the ignorance and the greed, which made this horror possible.

Franklin Roosevelt, American President

我们必须尽一切努力战胜怀疑与恐惧、无知与贪婪，那是产生可怕的战争的根源。

——富兰克林·罗斯福，美国总统

Peace hath her victories no less renowned than war.

John Milton, British poet

和平的胜利与战争的胜利一样辉煌。

——弥尔顿，英国诗人

Franklin Roosevelt

富兰克林·罗斯福（1882—1945），美国政治家和第32届总统（1933—1945）。他生于纽约州，1907年成为律师，后从政。1932年，他提出“新政”计划以应对经济危机，使国家复苏。他是唯一连任三届的美国总统，也是美国历史上唯一一位残疾人总统。他试图使美国免于卷入二战未果，遂修正美国中立立场支援盟国，因珍珠港事件宣布参战。他曾在德黑兰和雅尔塔会晤丘吉尔和斯大林。

John Milton

弥尔顿（1608—1674），英国诗人。他生于伦敦，曾在剑桥大学学习，后来在霍顿苦读六年，为他后来成为诗人做准备。他用拉丁文写的诗歌早已使他颇有名气。1652年他双目失明，随后投身于诗歌创作，成为仅次于莎士比亚并广泛受到尊敬的诗人。其代表作有杰出的宗教史诗《失乐园》、《复乐园》、《力士参孙》及著名的《论出版自由》。

That misunderstandings and neglect create more confusion in this world than trickery and malice.

Goethe, German writer

世上由误解和疏忽而造成的纷乱要比奸猾和恶意造成的更多。

——歌德，德国作家

Man tends to increase at a greater rate than his means of subsistence; consequently he is occasionally subjected to a severe struggle for existence.

Charles Darwin, British biologist

人类的增长速度往往比生存手段提高得更快，因此人类有时不得不为生存进行激烈的斗争。

——达尔文，英国生物学家

First keep peace within yourself, then you can also bring peace to others.

Thomas Mann, German writer

首先要自己维护和平，然后才能给别人带来和平。

——托马斯·曼，德国作家

A peace is the nature of a conquest; for then both parties nobly are subdued, and neither party loser.

William Shakespeare, British dramatist

和平本身就是一种胜利，因为双方都是光荣的屈服者，谁也没有失败。

——莎士比亚，英国剧作家

It takes at least two to make a peace, but one can make a war.

Neville Chamberlain, British statesman

和平需要双方共同努力,但是一方就可以挑起战争。

——张伯伦,英国政治家

Truths
真理

Truth is the foundation and justification for perfection and beauty.

Francis Bacon, British essayist and philosopher

真是善和美赖以存在的基础和依据。

——培根,英国散文作家、哲学家

Eternal truths will be neither true nor eternal unless they have fresh meaning for every new social situation.

Franklin Roosevelt, American President

永恒的真理如果不在新的社会形势下赋予新的意义,要么它就不是真理,要么就不是永恒的。

——罗斯福,美国总统

The deepest truths are the simplest and the most common.

F. W. Robertson, British clergyman

最深刻的真理是最简单和最平凡的。

——罗伯森,英国牧师

Truth is on the march; nothing can stop it now.

Zola, French novelist

真理来了,什么也阻挡不了。

——左拉,法国小说家

No object is mysterious. The mystery is your eye.

Elizabeth Bourne, British female writer

万物皆非神秘,神秘的是你的眼光。

——伊丽莎白·伯恩,英国女作家

He who possesses most must be most afraid of loss.

Leonardo da Vinci, Italian painter

拥有最多的人也最害怕失去。

——达·芬奇,意大利画家

Truth is the property of no individual but is the treasure of all men.

Ralph Waldo Emerson, American thinker

真理不是某个人的资产,而是人类共同享有的财富。

——爱默生,美国思想家

It is indeed desirable to be well descended, but the glory belongs to our ancestors.

Plutarch, Ancient Greek historian and philosopher

出身名门当然好,但名门的光荣属于先辈。

——普鲁塔克,古希腊历史学家、哲学家

Irrationally held truths may be more harmful than reasoned errors.

T. Huxley, British biologist

盲目坚持的真理比理性的错误危害更大。

——赫胥黎,英国生物学家

Homer

荷马（约公元前9世纪），古希腊诗人，两部伟大的史诗：描述特洛伊围城故事的《伊利亚特》和讲述尤利西斯漫游经历的《奥德塞》据信都出自他的手笔。他的出生地至今未能确定。人们长期以来一直争论不休，有的认为荷马史诗出自他一人之手，有的则认为是后人根据荷马及其后裔世代口头相传的叙事诗记录整理的作品，但是有一点基本可以肯定，荷马史诗植根于当时流行的民谣，是经作者刻意润色和补充之后的作品。关于真实的荷马，我们所知的都是不确定的。

Marcus Tullius Cicero

西塞罗（公元前106—公元前43年），古罗马演说家、政治家、作家。他生于拉丁姆，在罗马学习法律、雄辩术、哲学和文学，最后走上了政治道路。他指出人们为相互保护而达成了契约，由此产生了政府。他提出了法律是世界自然状态的产物，用以保证人皆享有的权利。他的思想对罗马法律的发展，对后来西方民主与法学思想的发展，产生了重大影响。

Love truth, but pardon error.

Voltaire, French thinker

热爱真理,但应宽恕错误。

——伏尔泰,法国思想家

Time, whose tooth paws away everything else, is powerless against truth.

T. Huxley, British biologist

时间的利齿可以吞噬一切别的东西,对真理却无能为力。

——赫胥黎,英国生物学家

Power without wisdom will always lead to certain disaster. But wisdom will bring you not only its own delights but power as well.

Homer, Ancient Greek poet

没有智慧的权力总是要导致灾难,但如果你得到智慧,它不仅会给你带来欢乐,也给你带来权力。

——荷马,古希腊诗人

Only in states in which the power of the people is supreme has liberty any abode.

Marcus Tullius Cicero, Ancient Roman statesman and orator

只有在人民的权力是至高无上的国度里,自由才有栖身之地。

——西塞罗,古罗马政治家、演说家

You can fool all the people some of the time, and some of the people all the time, but you cannot fool all the people all the time.

Abraham Lincoln, American President

你可能在某个时候愚弄所有的人,也可能一直在愚弄某些人,但是你不可能在所有的时候愚弄所有的人。

——林肯,美国总统

Democracy

民主

Liberty is the right to do everything, which the laws allow.

Montesquieu, French philosopher and jurist

自由即有权做法律所许可的一切事情。

——孟德斯鸠,法国哲学家、法理学家

It is conflict and not unquestioning agreement that keeps freedom alive. In a free country there will always be conflicting ideas, and this is a source of strength.

Thomas Jefferson, American President

使自由保持活力的是冲突,而不是绝对的一致。在一个自由的国家里总会有冲突的思想,而这正是力量的源泉。

——杰斐逊,美国总统

Smokers and nonsmokers cannot be equally free in the same railway carriage.

George Bernard Shaw, British dramatist

吸烟者和不吸烟者无法在同一节车厢里享受同样的自由。

——萧伯纳,英国剧作家

Fact of the matter is, there is no hip world, and there is no straight world. There's a world, you see, which has people in it who believe in a variety of different things. Everybody believes in something and everybody, by virtue of the fact that they believe in something, uses that something to support their own existence.

Frank Zappa,
American master of Rock and Roll

事实上,既没有新潮世界,也没有老派世界。我们只有一个世界,在这个世界里人们执有不同的观点,人们有这样那样的信仰,并凭借其信仰而生存。

——弗兰克·扎帕,美国摇滚大师

We hold these truths to be self-evident: that all men are created equal; that they are endowed by their creator with certain unalienable rights; that among these are life, liberty, and the pursuit of happiness.

Thomas Jefferson, American President

我们认为这些真理是不言而喻的:人人生而平等;他们被造物主赋予某些不可让与的权利,其中包括生活、自由和追求幸福的权利。

——杰斐逊,美国总统

Absolute freedom mocks at justice. Absolute justice denies freedom.

Albert Camus, French writer

绝对的自由是对公正的嘲弄。绝对的公正是对自由的否定。

——加缪,法国作家

Frank Zappa

弗兰克·扎帕（1940—1993），美国摇滚大师。1940年，他出生于美国巴尔的摩，1960年出版了第一张唱片，是一部电影的插曲。在此后的音乐生涯中，扎帕推出多张专辑，1969年以个人专辑《热鼠》获得“出色的爵士摇滚音乐家”的称号。扎帕1979年推出经典作品《Joe's Garage Act 1》，扎帕在1993年12月去世，之前一直创作不止，是美国20世纪60年代摇滚乐发展史上的先锋人物之一，被公认为是一位摇滚大师。

Albert Camus

加缪（1913—1960），法国存在主义作家。他生于阿尔及利亚的蒙多维，曾在阿尔及尔大学学习哲学。自1935年起，他开始从事戏剧活动，曾创办剧团，扮演过许多角色。法国解放后，他与萨特共同主编左翼报纸《战斗报》。他的虚无主义小说《局外人》为其赢得了国际声誉。其后期作品有《鼠疫》、《堕落》，他还写过戏剧和几部政治著作。他于1957年获得诺贝尔文学奖。

Thomas Jefferson

杰斐逊（1743—1826），美国政治家和第三任总统。他生于弗吉尼亚州，1767年取得律师资格，后参加革命党派，并参与起草了《独立宣言》。他曾历任弗吉尼亚州长、驻法国大使、国务卿、亚当斯总统的副总统，直至就任总统。他任期内的重大事件有与的黎波里的战争、购买路易斯安那和禁止奴隶贸易。他在建筑、自然科学、人文科学和教育等领域均有极深的造诣。

If democracy is to survive, it is the task of men of thoughts, as well as men of action, to put aside pride and prejudice; and with courage and single-minded devotion—to find the truth and teach the truth that shall keep men free.

Franklin Roosevelt, American President

若想有民主,人们在思想和行动上就须摒弃傲慢与偏见;他们要有勇气,有全心全意的献身精神,最重要的是要有谦虚精神,去寻求并传播那些使人民永葆自由的真理。

——罗斯福,美国总统

Unless it goes hand in hand with science, democracy will have no future.

Maxim Gorky, Russian writer

民主只有与科学携手共进,才能有未来。

——高尔基,俄国作家

If national pride is ever justifiable or excusable it is when it springs, not from power or riches, grandeur or glory, but from conviction of national innocence, information, and benevolence.

John Adams, American President

如果说民族自豪感历来无可非议和情有可原,那么,这种自豪感就不是来自权势和财富,不是来自豪华和荣耀,而是来自坚信民族的纯真、见识和仁爱。

——亚当斯,美国总统

The history of liberty is a history of the limitation of government power.

Woodrow Wilson, American President

自由的历史就是限制政府权力的历史。

——威尔逊，美国总统

Liberty is the only thing you cannot have unless you give it to others.

William A. White, American journalist

自由，你不给予别人你自己也无法获得。

——怀特，美国记者

Nothing is more precious than independence and freedom.

Ho Chi Minh, Vietnamese statesman

没有什么比独立和自由更为宝贵。

——胡志明，越南政治家

Wherever in the world a people know desperate want, there must appear at least the spark of hope, the hope of progress—or there will surely raise at last the flames of conflict.

Dwight D. Eisenhower, Commander in Chief of the Allied forces in the Second World War

任何地方，一个民族只要知道自己迫切需要什么，那里就会出现希望的火花，出现进步的希望，换句话说，最后必定会燃起抗争的火焰。

——艾森豪威尔，二战中盟军最高司令

Politics
政治

History is past politics, and politics is present history.

Sir Ralph Freeman, British engineer

历史是过去的政治,政治是现在的历史。

——弗里曼爵士,英国工程师

Those people who treat politics and morality separately will never understand either of them.

Rousseau, French thinker

若把政治和道德割裂开来,那就既不懂得政治,亦不理解道德。

——卢梭,法国思想家

Politics is perhaps the only profession for which no preparation is thought necessary.

Robert Louis Stevenson, British novelist

也许政治是唯一不必作任何准备就能从事的职业。

——史蒂文森,英国小说家

No state can pledge its future to another.

Heinrich Von Treitschke, German historian

任何国家都不能把自己的未来托付给别的国家。

——特莱奇克,德国历史学家

The greatness of a country does not depend on its size but on the quality of its citizens and the leadership.

Kjarval, Gambia statesman

一个国家的伟大并不看它的幅员大小,而要看它的公民及其领导的素质。

——贾瓦拉,冈比亚政治家

War is nothing but a continuation of politics with the admixture of other means.

Carl von Clausewitz, Prussian General

战争不过是政治的延续,外加一些别的手段。

——克劳塞威茨,普鲁士将军

The greater the power, the more dangerous the abuse.

Edmund Burke, British statesman

权力越大,滥用的危险就越大。

——伯克,英国政治家

They have rights who dare maintain them.

James Russell Lowell, American poet and diplomat

敢于坚持权力,就享有权力。

——詹姆斯·洛威尔,美国诗人、外交家

We need in politics men who have some thing to give, not men who have something to get.

Bernard Baruch, American economist

政治需要有所奉献的人,而不是想有所收获的人。

——巴鲁克,美国经济学家

George Washington

乔治·华盛顿（1732—1799），美利坚合众国第一任总统。他出生于弗吉尼亚州，在当地的政治活动中享有盛名。他任弗吉尼亚州议会议员，并出席了两届大陆会议，在独立战争中任殖民地军总司令。战争结束后，他退隐山庄，寻求依靠宪法确保建立一个坚强政府的办法，在费城召开的制宪会议中他被推举为主席，他的人格力量促使废除十三州联邦宪法代之以一个激进的新宪法，1789 年被代表们一致推选为美利坚合众国第一任总统。

Charles de Gaulle

戴高乐（1890—1970），法国将军和第五共和国第一任总统。他生于法国里尔，曾在圣西尔军校学习，成绩优异。他参加过第一次世界大战，极力主张机械化战争。二战期间，当法国政府准备同德国谈判停战时，戴高乐离开法国前往英国，举起“自由法国”的旗帜。此后，他作为自由法兰西武装力量的领袖，带领人民积极反抗纳粹德国。北非动乱后（1958），戴高乐当选为法兰西共和国总统。1965 年，他成为首任通过全民普选当选的总统，被认为是战后最为鼓舞人心的领导人。戴高乐执政期间奉行独立自主的外交政策，极力同第三世界国家发展关系，使法国成为当时西方国家中第一个同中国建立大使级外交关系的国家。戴高乐为维护法国的独立和主权，为维护世界和平作出了卓越的贡献。

When a man assumes a public trust, he should consider himself as public property.

Thomas Jefferson, American President

当一个人受到公众信任时,他就应该把自己看作公众的财产。

——杰斐逊,美国总统

All politics are based on the indifference of the majority.

James Reston, American editor

一切政治都是建立在多数人冷漠的基础上的。

——赖斯顿,美国编辑

The administration of justice is the firmest pillar of government.

George Washington, American President

主持正义是政府最坚定的支柱。

——华盛顿,美国总统

Since a politician never believes what he says, he is surprised when others believe him.

Charles de Gaulle, French President

政客从来不相信自己说的话,所以当别人相信他的话时,他必定会大吃一惊。

——戴高乐,法国总统

The government of the people, by the people, and for the people shall not perish from the Earth.

Abraham Lincoln, American President

民有、民治、民享的政府永世长存。

——林肯,美国总统

Public officers are the servants and agents of the people, to execute the laws which the people have made.

Grover Cleveland, American President

政府官员是人民的公仆和代理人,执行人民制定的法律。

——克利夫兰,美国总统

Beneath the rule of men entirely great, the pen is mightier than the sword.

Lytton, British writer and statesman

伟人的法则是,笔比剑更有力。

——利顿,英国作家、政治家

No government can be long secure without a formidable opposition.

Benjamin Disraeli, British statesman

没有一个难以对付的反对党,任何政府都不能长期稳定。

——狄斯累利,英国政治家

Law
法律

The law cannot make all men equal, but they are all equal before the law.

Frederick Pollock, British jurist

法律不能使人人平等,但是在法律面前人人平等。

——波洛克,英国法理学家

Laws grind the poor, and rich men rule the law.

Oliver Goldsmith, British writer

法律折磨穷人,而富人却掌握法律。

——戈德史密斯,英国作家

Law is order, and good law is good order.

Aristotle, Ancient Greek philosopher

法律就是秩序,有好的法律才有好的秩序。

——亚里士多德,古希腊哲学家

Law can never be enforced unless fear supports it.

Sophocles, Ancient Greek dramatist

法律如果没有恐惧支撑,绝不能生效。

——索福克勒斯,古希腊剧作家

Good order is the foundation of all things.

Edmund Burke, British statesman

良好的秩序是一切事物的基础。

——伯克,英国政治家

Laws are generally found to be nets of such a texture, as the little creep through, the great break through, and the middle-sized are alone entangled in.

William Shenstone, British poet

人们通常会发现,法律就是这样一种网,触犯法律的人,小的可以穿网而过,大的可以破网而去,只有中等的才会坠入网中。

——申斯通,英国诗人

The greatest happiness of the greatest number is the foundation of morals and legislation.

Jeremy Bentham,
British philosopher and social reformer

维护最大多数人的最大幸福是道德和立法的基础。

——边沁,英国哲学家、社会改革家

Religion
宗教

The scriptures teach us the best way of living, the noblest way of suffering, and the most comfortable way of dying.

John Flavel, American theologian

《圣经》教给我们最好的生活方式、苦难中最高尚的做法、死亡时最放松的办法。

——约翰·弗拉维尔，美国神学家

Without philosophy man cannot know what he makes; without religion he cannot know why.

Eril Gill, British sculptor

没有哲学，人们不可能知道自己创造了什么；没有宗教，人们不知道为什么去创造。

——吉尔，英国雕塑家

Whom the God wish to destroy, the first made mad.

Euripiedes, Ancient Greek dramatist

上帝要谁灭亡，必先让他疯狂。

——欧里庇得斯，古希腊剧作家

God dwells wherever man lets him in.

Mendel of Kotzk

上帝住在人允许他进去的所有地方。

——科策克的门德尔

Economy
经济

Taxes are what we pay for civilized society.

O. W. Holmes, American physician and writer

税是我们为文明社会所付出的代价。

——霍尔姆斯，美国医生、作家

Information is power; the information domain is the future battlefield.

Cebrows Arthur, American economist

信息就是力量，信息领域是未来的战场。

——阿瑟，美国经济学家

No country, however rich, can afford the waste of its human resources.

Franklin Roosevelt, American President

一个国家不管多么富裕，都浪费不起人力资源。

——罗斯福，美国总统

There is no resting place for an enterprise in a competitive economy.

Alfred P. Sloan, American businessman

在竞争的经济中，没有企业休息的地方。

——斯隆，美国实业家

A beautiful woman is paradise for the eyes, hell for the soul, and purgatory for the purse.

Nicolas Chamfort, French writer

美女是眼睛的天堂、灵魂的地狱、钱包的炼狱。

——尚福，法国作家

Technology is like fish. The longer it stays on the shelf, the less desirable it becomes.

Andrew Heller, American IBM executive of IBM

技术就像鱼，在货架上放的时间越长越没人要。

——赫勒，美国 IBM 公司执行官

Computers make it easier to do a lot of things, but most of the things they make it easier to do don't need to be done.

Andy Rooney, American columnist

计算机使许多工作做起来更容易，但其中大多数都是没有必要做的。

——安迪·鲁尼，美国专栏作家

It shouldn't be too much of a surprise that the internet has evolved into a force strong enough to reflect the greatest hopes and fears of those who use it.

Denise Caruso,

American digital commerce columnist

一点儿也不奇怪，互联网已经发展成为如此强大的力量，足以反映那些用户们最大的希望和恐惧。

——卡鲁索，美国数字商业专栏作家

Marshall McLuhan

麦克卢汉（1911—1980），加拿大传媒学家，出生于加拿大艾伯塔省埃德蒙顿市。1951 年，麦克卢汉第一本专著《机器新娘》出版，这本书广泛分析报纸、广播、电影和广告产生的社会冲击和心理影响，但没有产生多大的影响。接着，他相继出版了《谷登堡星光璀璨》、《理解媒介》，一时间令人叹为观止，在人文学科领域引起了强烈震撼。他独自孵化出了一种全新的思想：他潜心研究媒介传播、电脑等电子技术的社会影响和对人类的心理影响。在 20 世纪 60 年代，麦克卢汉被认为是自牛顿、达尔文和爱因斯坦以来最重要的思想家。他一直是个有影响力和有争议的人物，他提出的“媒介即是讯息”（the medium is the message）、地球村（global village）等已常挂在人们的嘴边。他被认为是电子时代的先驱和预言家，媒介理论的奠基人。如今，他的预言一个个变成了现实，他所谓的“意识延伸”就是信息网络、虚拟现实，他所谓的“地球村”已然到来。

John Maynard Keynes

凯恩斯（1883—1946），现代西方经济学最有影响力的经济学家之一。他出身于英国一个学者家庭，大学期间，他已体现出冷静而又合乎逻辑的思想和优秀的道德标准，顺利获得数学硕士学位。此后，凯恩斯的兴趣转到经济学。1914 年第一次世界大战拉开帷幕，英国爆发经济危机，此时身在剑桥的凯恩斯被任命为财政部要员，使迫在眉睫的经济恐慌得以缓解。1921 年，他出版了《概率论》。该书体现了他深邃的哲学思想和高超的逻辑演绎能力。1929 年，资本主义世界爆发了有史以来最严重的经济危机，凯恩斯再度挺身而出，发表了《利息就业和货币通论》，解释了危机发生的根本原因及其解决办法，引发了一次经济思想革命，史称“凯恩斯革命”。1944 年，他出席布雷顿森林联合国货币金融会议，并担任了国际货币基金组织和国际复兴开发银行的董事。1946 年，他猝死于心脏病，时年 63 岁。凯恩斯一生对经济学作出了极大的贡献，一度享有资本主义的“救星”、“战后繁荣之父”等美称。

If enterprise is afoot, wealth accumulates whatever may be happening to thrift; and if enterprise is asleep, wealth decays, whatever thrift may be doing.

John Maynard Keynes, British economist

如果企业在发展,不论节俭与否,财富都在积聚;如果企业停滞不前,不论节俭与否,财富都在锐减。

——凯恩斯,英国经济学家

It is Enterprise which builds and improves the world's possessions. Thrift may be the handmaid and nurse of Enterprise. But equally she may not. For the engine which drives Enterprise is not Thrift, but Profit.

John Maynard Keynes, British economist

进取精神建造了和增加了世界上的财富。节俭可以是进取精神的仆人和护理人,同样地也可以不是。因为进取精神的动力不是节俭,而是利润。

——凯恩斯,英国经济学家

The new electronic interdependence recreates the world in the image of global village.

Marshall McLuhan,
Canadian Scholar and communications theorist

新的电子连接和依存将世界变成了地球村。

——麦克卢汉,加拿大学者、传播学理论家

There can be no economy where there is no efficiency.

Disraeli, British statesman

没有效率就没有经济。

——迪斯累利,英国政治家

Enthusiasm for a medium that keeps you away from human beings strikes me as worrying.

Ian Hislop,
editor of the British satirical magazine Private Eye

人们对一种让人远离他人的媒介的热衷让我震惊,令我担忧。

——伊恩·希斯洛普,
英国讽刺杂志《私家侦探》主编

我喜欢的名人名言

Some of my favorite quotes that are not contained in this book are:

我喜欢的名人名言

Some of my favorite quotes that are not contained in this book are:

有奖阅读

我们的心愿是希望阅读我们的图书能使您有所受益，那么读完这本书，您有什么收获呢？试着回答下面这些问题，来加深对这本书的印象吧，所有的答案均可以在本书中找到哦！

1. 阿拉伯第一个文学流派是________________。
2. 剧本《奇迹创造者》的主人公是________________。
3. Emerson 毕业于________________大学。
4. 集体无意识理论是________________提出的。
5. 《魔鬼辞典》的作者是________________。
6. “希腊三贤”指的是：__________、__________、__________。
7. “诺贝尔奖金”共涉及几个领域？请一一列出：

__________、__________、__________、__________、__________、__________。

8. 压强的国际符号 Pa，是用________________的名字命名的。
9. All Men Are Brothers 是我国哪部名著的英译本名称？________________。
10. 美国宾夕法尼亚的创建人是________________。
11. 最先采用称作“托德—AO”的三维宽银幕电影技术拍摄影片的是________________。
12. “产业革命”一词是由________________最早提出的。
13. Charles Colton uses the word “sound” in chapter Friendship, Jules Combarie uses the word “sound” in chapter Culture, which of the “sounds” can be used in the sentence of “He’s in a sound sleep”?
14. 书中共介绍了几位诺贝尔奖金获得者？

将您的答案填好，与下页的读者调查表一并寄给我们，您将有机会获得精美礼品一份。

邮寄地址：山西省太原市郝庄邮政4505信箱

邮政编码：030045　　E-mail: quotation.syl@163.com

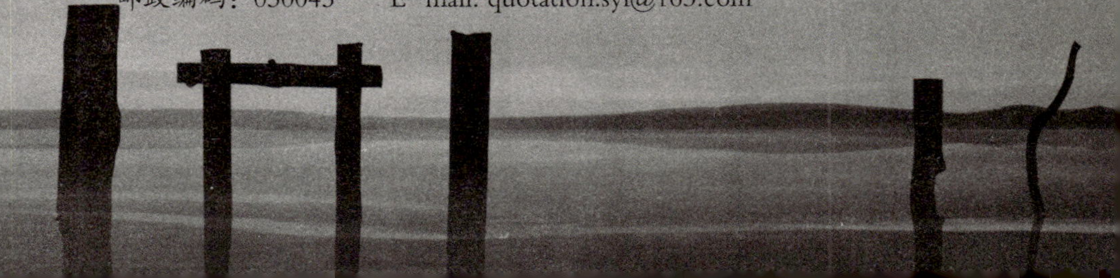

读者调查表

亲爱的读者朋友：

为了深入地了解您的阅读状况，优化图书选题，出版更加符合读者阅读兴趣的图书，我们设计了这份调查表，希望听到来自您的真实声音，以便我们不断提高图书品质，使读者真正获益！您所填写的内容仅作为研究分析之用，个人资料绝对保密。

（以下题目可以多选）

1. 您平时喜欢阅读哪一类书籍以提高自己的文化修养？

□ 中国古典文学作品　□ 世界优秀文学作品　□ 艺术类书籍

□ 其他（请注明 ____________________）

2. 您平时喜欢阅读哪一类书籍以开阔自己的视野？

□ 名人传记　□ 历史地理　□ 财经时事　□ 军事政治　□ 科普读物

□ 其他（请注明 ____________________）

3. 您平时喜欢阅读哪一类读物来进行英语学习？

□ 纯英文读物　□ 中英文对照读物　□ 英语教辅读物　□ 英语视听读物

□ 其他（请注明 ____________________）

4. 您喜欢通过什么渠道来购买图书？

□ 网上订阅　□ 书店挑选　□ 老师或朋友推荐　□ 其他（请注明 ______________）

5. 您是如何读到本书的？

□ 自己购买　□ 老师或朋友推荐　□ 赠阅　□ 其他（请注明 ______________）

6. 您觉得本书最吸引您的是什么？

7. 您觉得本书的不足之处在哪里？

8. 您对我们的其他意见和建议。

让我们认识你：

姓名：__________　性别：________　年龄：_______　您的职业：__________

联系电话：__________________　您的业余爱好：________________

您的地址：____

邮政编码：__________________　E-mail：________________________